Sydney Strolls

☼ EASTERN SUBURBS

Dedicated to John Horbury Hunt and to Professor Leslie Wilkinson for designing so many elegant and aesthetically pleasing buildings in the eastern suburbs.

Sydney Strolls

EASTERN SUBURBS

NEW HOLLAND

Graham Spindler

By the same author
Sydney Strolls: Lower North Shore (1999)

First published in Australia in 1999 by
New Holland Publishers (Australia) Pty Ltd
Sydney • Auckland • London • Cape Town

14 Aquatic Drive, Frenchs Forest NSW 2086, Australia
218 Lake Road, Northcote Auckland, New Zealand
24 Nutford Place, London W1H 6DQ, United Kingdom
80 McKenzie Street, Cape Town 8001 South Africa

Copyright © 1999 in text: Graham Spindler
Copyright © 1999 in maps: New Holland Publishers (Australia) Pty Ltd
Copyright © 1999 in photographs: Graham Spindler
Copyright © 1999 New Holland Publishers (Australia) Pty Ltd

All rights reserved. No part of this publication may be reproduced, stored in a retrieval system or transmitted, in any form or by any means, electronic, mechanical, photocopying, recording or otherwise, without the prior written permission of the publishers and copyright holders.

National Library of Australia Cataloguing-in-Publication Data:

Spindler, Graham.
Sydney Strolls: Eastern Suburbs

ISBN 1 86436 400 9
1. Walking — New South Wales — Sydney — Guidebooks. 2. Hiking — New South Wales — Sydney — Guidebooks. 3. Sydney (N.S.W.) — Tours. I. Title.

919.4410466

Project Manager: Fiona Doig
Editor: Emma Wise
Maps illustrated by: Di Bradley
Design and layout by: Tricia McCallum
Printer: Times Printers, Malaysia

Cover illustration from the original painting 'Nielsen Park, Vaucluse'
by Erin Hill of Erin Hill Gallery. © 1999.

Contents

Acknowledgments **7**

Regional map **8**

Introduction **10**

Cross Currents
Kings Cross, Potts Point, Elizabeth Bay
Feature: Goodbye Bohemia
11

Social Climbing
Bondi Junction, Bellevue Hill, Woollahra, Edgecliff
Feature: The Baronet of Woollahra
32

A Touch of Class
Darling Point
Feature: Swamp Stories
18

Hermitage Heritage
Rose Bay, Nielsen Park, Vaucluse
Feature: Boats that Flew
38

Arsenals & Old Lace
Paddington
Feature: The Barracks
25

Commanding Heights
Vaucluse
Feature: Wentworth of Vaucluse
45

Walls of Stone
Watsons Bay
Feature: Sir John & the Head Scientist
52

Beaches 1
Bondi, Tamarama, Bronte
Feature: Beach Couture
59

Beaches 2
Bronte, Clovelly, Coogee
Feature: The Case of the Shark's Arm
65

Racing Through
Randwick
Feature: Randwick Revisited—Simeon Pearce
71

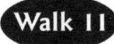

Homes & Gardens
Daceyville
Feature: Bungalow Building
78

Dangerous Coast
Little Bay, Cape Banks
Feature: Shipwrecked!
85

Inside Henry's Head
La Perouse, Botany Bay National Park
Feature: La Per
91

Acknowledgments

Many people help make a book. Laraine, my wife, and my daughters, Meg and Seonha, treated with great tolerance (and, quite possibly, appreciation) my frequent and extended disappearances in an easterly direction or into the study. Fellow walkers and friends contributed information, ideas, road tests and enthusiasm. Dozens of writers, local historians and photographers who had been there before me, along with staff in public libraries and local government, provided so many of the raw materials and insights that made exploration of the eastern suburbs exciting and rewarding for me.

The photos are my own. Thanks to Fiona Doig at New Holland for suggesting that I do the book and to Fiona and the team who made it happen—including Tricia McCallum for the book design, Di Bradley for the maps, Erin Hill for the cover illustration and Emma Wise for the invaluable and rigorous editing.

13 Walks in the Eastern Suburbs

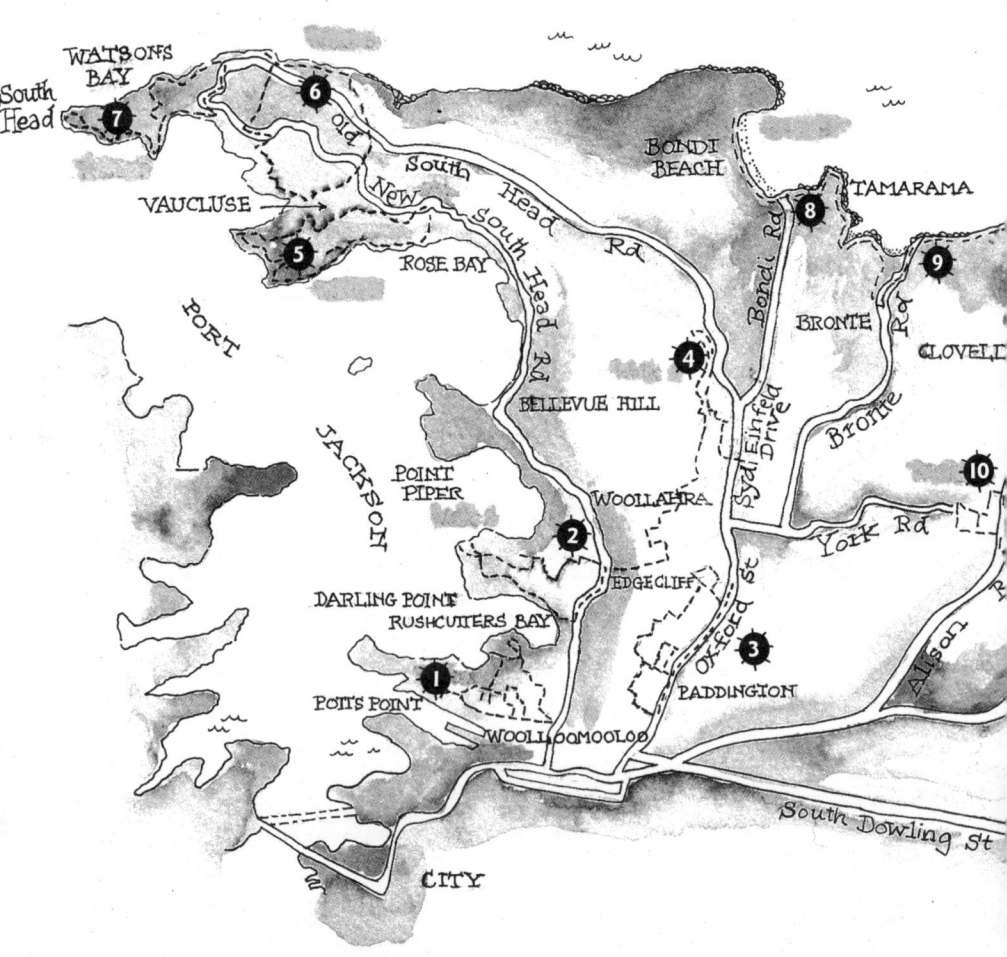

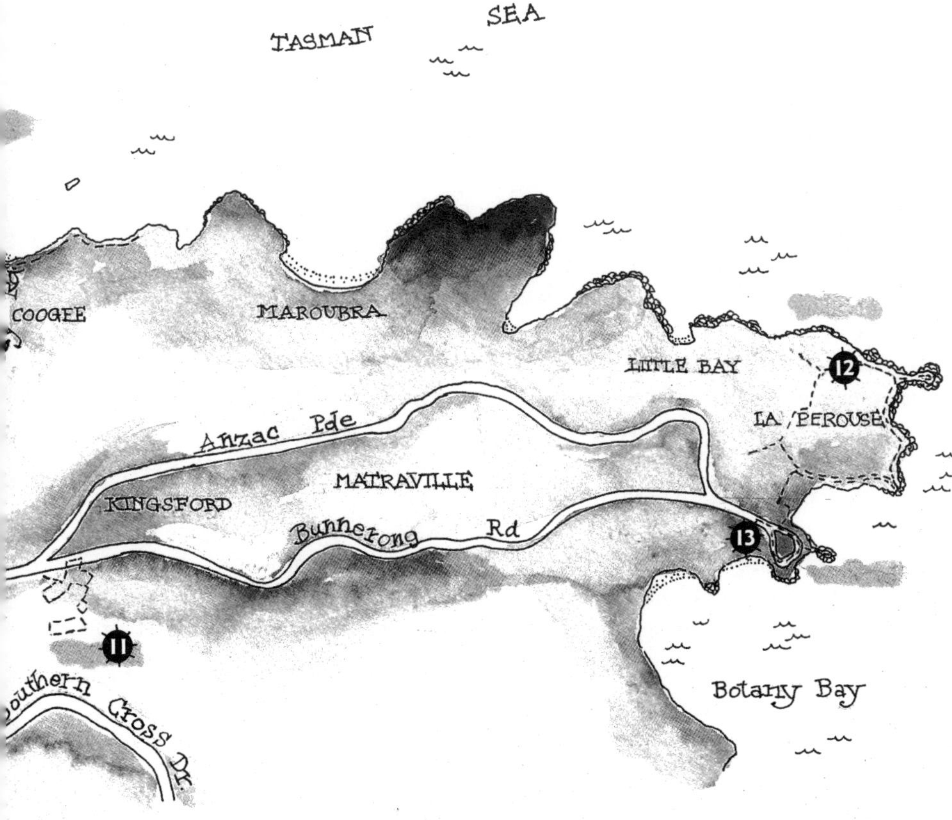

TASMAN SEA
COOGEE
MAROUBRA
LITTLE BAY
LA PEROUSE
Anzac Pde
MATRAVILLE
KINGSFORD
Bunnerong Rd
12
13
11
Southern Cross Dr.
Botany Bay

Introduction

Sydney is one of the worlds' great walking cities. Its eastern suburbs offer diverse and often magnificent scenery with beaches, bays, cliffs and natural landscapes mingling with some of Sydney's most relaxed lifestyles, expensive real estate and impressive domestic architecture. Once rocky harboursides, ocean headlands or sandy shrublands, it is now intensely settled. Yet through design, accident and military requirement, much of its natural environment remains, amidst a built environment with many features that contribute interest, utility and grace.

The 13 walks take place across the broad geographic and social spectrum of the area, which I define as bounded by the coastline from South Head to Botany Bay, then back from Sydney Airport along the airport motorway to about Garden Island and thence along the harbour foreshores back to South Head. And beyond these walks, there is much more to explore in the east. Try the coastline south of Maroubra; Point Piper; Bellevue Hill; Queen and Ocean Streets, Woollahara; Centennial Park; or Waverley and Botany Cemeteries. Eastern suburbs real estate may cost the Earth but it is free to those who take the time to walk through it.

As an aside to each walk chapter, a feature box expands on an essential or esoteric matter linked to the walk: bikinis, baronets, bohemians, and bungalows; or shipwrecks, sharks, seaplanes and swamps.

Each walk begins with some summary information: **main features** (architecture, history, bushland, etc); **how long** the walk is in length and **time** (most are between one-and-a-half and three hours). Times are really up to you but they do not include visits to historic houses or museums where these appear. **Levels of difficulty and accessibility** are suggested— no walks are really difficult for people of average fitness, but there are often heart-pumping steps and inclines. Adventurous stroller pushers can manage many parts of the walks; but wheelchair access is much more restricted.

The maps and **access information** includes some public transport information, and map references for the starting points come from the UBD and Gregory's street directories, 1998 or 1999 editions. Toilets, shops and picnic spots are listed under **Facilities**. **Dogs** must be kept out of the National Parks (Walks 5, 7, 12 and 13). The **maps** highlight several features in each walk—sometimes because of their importance, but mostly to provide a check that you are in the right place. There are always lots of interesting features that don't get shown on the map to avoid overcrowding! One or two suggestions for **additional reading** are provided for each walk. Of course, when you walk, wear a hat and plenty of sunscreen lotion, good walking shoes, and take your own water with you, especially on hotter days.

And I hope that this book contributes to your enjoyment and discovery of Sydney's exhilarating eastern suburbs.

Walk 1

Cross Currents

Kings Cross, Potts Point, Elizabeth Bay

This walk covers three neighbourhoods that rub shoulders with each other, yet retain distinct characters. It begins at Kings Cross, near the road junction atop William Street. Called Queens Cross in 1897 to mark Queen Victoria's Diamond Jubilee, the name was changed (with a King on the throne) eight years later.

Additional Reading
Elizabeth Butel & Tom Thompson *Kings Cross Album*, Atrand, Sydney, 1984.
Memories of Kings Cross 1936–1946, Kings Cross Community Aid & Information Service, 1981.

Background: *Crossroads of the world—Kings Cross and the El Alamein Fountain.*

Features
Wide-ranging domestic and historic architecture and streetscapes
• harbour views • naval base • social change • history.

Distance
Approx. 4½km return.

Time
2–3 hours.

Difficulty
Easy to moderate
• some steps • strollers OK • mostly wheelchair accessible.

Access
Kings Cross buses and rail • street parking (time restricted).
UBD: Map 4 C7
Gregory's: Map 4 H7.

Facilities
Toilets, picnic spots at Beare Park • shops, restaurants and hotels throughout.

12 ☼ Sydney Strolls ⚓ Eastern Suburbs

Walk 1 Key

- **S** Start
- **1** No. 202 Victoria St
- **2** Former Minerva Theatre
- **3** 'Tusculum'
- **4** St Vincents College
- **5** HMAS Kuttabul
- **6** 'Wyldefel Gardens'
- **7** Naval Maritime Headquarters
- **8** 'Rockwall'
- **9** Elizabeth Bay House
- **10** 'Boomerang'
- **11** 'Kincoppal'
- **12** 'Birtley Towers'

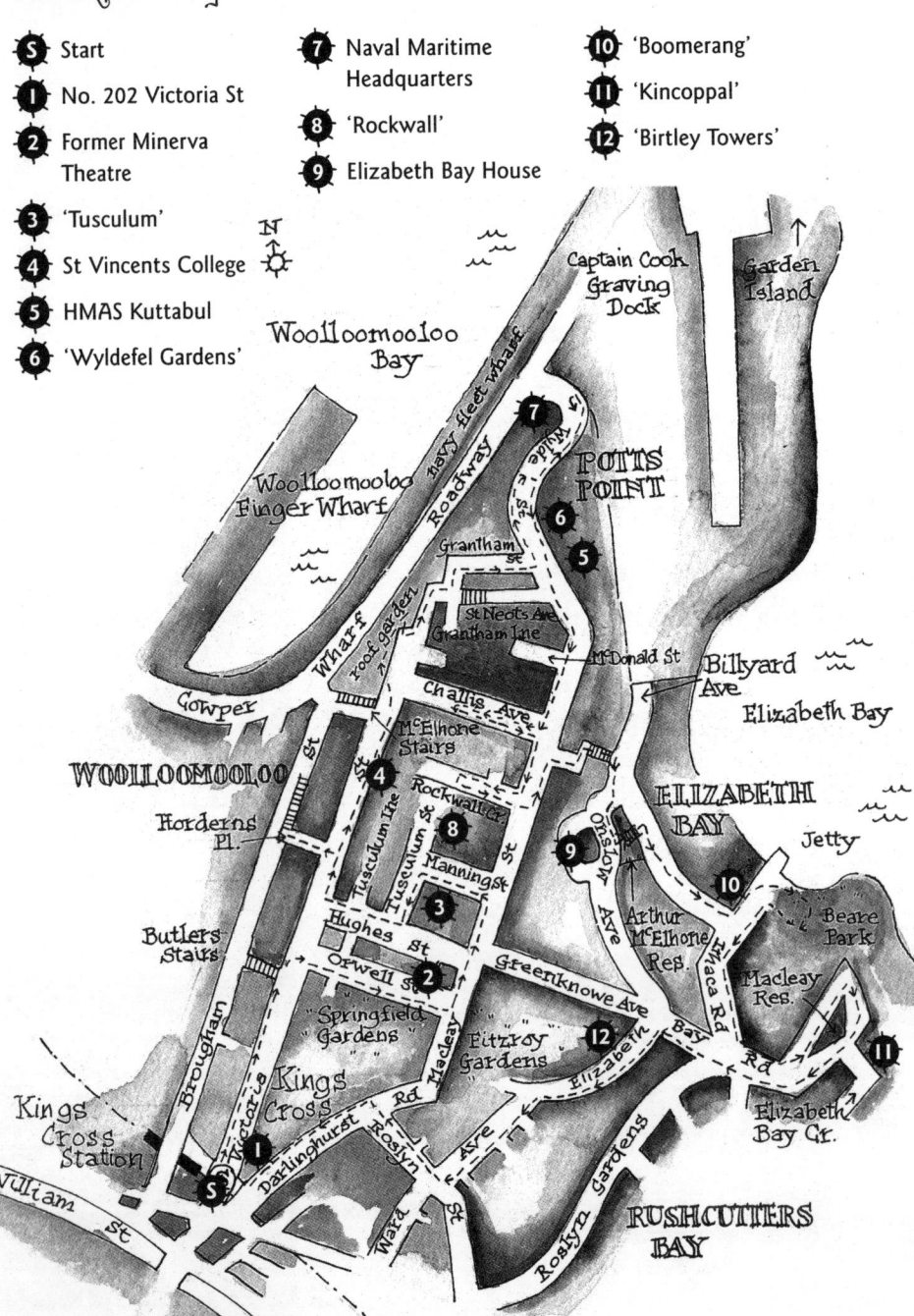

Kings Cross, Potts Point, Elizabeth Bay

The Cross—variously Sydney's seediest, liveliest, most colourful, notorious, bohemian, corrupt and cosmopolitan area—has seen many changes. By the 1920s it had a reputation for gunmen, crime, prostitution and gang wars, but was also becoming a bohemian landscape of flats and boarding houses, home to aspiring artists and intellectuals (see feature box, page 15). World War II brought the Americans and a brassier Cross and, although bohemia revived in the postwar decades, the Vietnam War and the 1970s and 80s changed the direction again.

The first European settlers in the area were leading public servants, judges, politicians, merchants—attracted to the ridge for fine town and harbour views. Governor Darling decreed a high standard for the Woolloomooloo Hill houses facing Sydney. By 1900 most of them had been subdivided or demolished, and terraced streets like Victoria Street had created the area's new character.

The walk begins at either of the two Victoria Street exits from Kings Cross railway station. Turn down Victoria Street towards the harbour. Hotels and high-rise quickly give way to an eclectic mix of stores, bookshops, backpacker hostels, plane trees and Victorian terraces of increasing elegance. Tiny **number 202** ❶ was home to local newspaper publisher Juanita Nielson, and a little further along on the city side are Butlers Stairs, with a memorial plaque to activist Mick Fowler. Both are reminders that Victoria Street in the early 1970s was the scene of a sustained and vicious development battle. Locals like Mick and Juanita were joined by the Builders' Labourers Federation and urban conservationists in using green bans, protests, site occupations and blockades to oppose the street's redevelopment into high-rise. Frustrated developers resorted to massive intimidation and force. Nielson, who supported the protests in her publication, disappeared without trace in July 1975. Ultimately, there was development, but the essential Victoria Street streetscape remains—a lasting monument to Juanita Nielson, Mick Fowler (who died in 1979) and the other battlers.

Cross Victoria Street from Butlers Stairs into Orwell Street. Opposite Springfield Gardens is the Art Deco former **Minerva (Metro) Theatre** ❷. A live theatre from 1938, its players included Peter Finch, Neva Carr-Glynne and Ron Randall. Converted into a fashionable movie theatre in the 1950s, it went live again in the 1960s with the archetypal hippy musical *Hair*, and later became a television production sound stage.

At Macleay Street turn left away from Kings Cross and walk down towards Potts Point. Take another left into Manning Street to **'Tusculum'** ❸. An indication of the grandeur that once was Potts Point, this 1830–32 simple Georgian Regency home—designed by John Verge for Alexander Brodie Spark—later had an upper verandah and other Victorian Italianate features added. Its first resident was Bishop Broughton, Australia's first Anglican Bishop. The house was restored in 1988 after a varied career as a hospital, hotel and even a World War II US Officers' Club. It now houses the Royal Australian Institute of Architects.

Continue via charming Tusculum and Hughes streets back to Victoria Street where tower blocks on the city side overshadow a mixture of late Victorian terraces and villas. Turn right and a little further on, between numbers 101 and 99 Victoria Street, Hordern Place takes you to the clifftop to appreciate both the expansive city view and the scale of the redevelopment behind the street frontages. Back on Victoria Street, heading towards the harbour, **St Vincent's College** 4 soon appears on the right. The Sisters of Charity purchased the mansion 'Tarmons' in 1856 from Sir Charles Nicholson (of the Nicholson Museum at Sydney University), beginning the college and St Vincent's Hospital here, though the latter moved to Darlinghurst in 1870.

Beyond McElhone Stairs, terraces give way to the large, mannered roof garden atop the Department of Defence Garden Island carpark. Overlooked by attractive Queen Anne terraces lining the eastern side of Victoria Street, this public park offers a view across the navy fleet wharf, usually arrayed with warships, towards the historic Woolloomooloo finger wharf, the Domain and the harbour. Barely in sight, nearby Garden Island was linked to Potts Point by the construction of Captain Cook Graving Dock during World War II. Between July 1940 and March 1945 an average of 3000 men worked around the clock reclaiming more than 13 hectares of harbour and building the dock, which is 346 metres long, 47 metres wide and 16 metres deep.

From the roof garden follow Grantham Lane, at the end of Victoria Street, to Grantham Street and along to the junction with Wylde Street. The 1960s flats opposite are the naval barracks **HMAS *Kuttabul*** 5, named after the depot ship (a former ferry) sunk at Garden Island during a Japanese midget submarine raid in May 1942. Nineteen young sailors died in the attack, as did the six crewmen of the three submarines (see Walks 4 and 7). The *Kuttabul* barracks occupy the site of 'Clarens', the once grand home and waterfront garden of Sir James Martin (1820–66), 19th-century Premier and Chief Justice of New South Wales—and the man Martin Place is named after (see Walk 9, page 65).

Almost everything north, west and east of this point was navy property by the end of World War II. Much has since been reprivatised, including **'Wyldefel Gardens'** 6, designed by its owner, W. A. Crowle, and the architect, John R. Brogan. Barely noticeable at street level a little further down Wylde Street towards the point, 'Wyldefel Gardens', with its two wings of flat-roofed garden apartments cascading down the hillside, was a landmark in modern Australian architecture when built in 1936. The original house, 'Wyldefel', now demolished, was once the home of Walter and Eliza Hall, who made their fortune in Cobb & Co. and mining, and used much of it to create medical research institutes.

The stone buildings at the bend in the road at the bottom of Wylde Street are part of **Naval Maritime Headquarters** 7, consisting of two houses more visible further downhill. 'Tarana' (1889) and the Italianate 'Bomera' (1856), the once grand homes of the McQuade family, went through the usual decline into boarding

Goodbye Bohemia

Small cheap flats, proximity to the city, coffee shops—rare in the bland Sydney of between the 1930s and 1960s—and an anything-goes reputation bought aspiring young arty-types flocking to the Cross. They created Australia's Bohemia, a living who's who of artists of the future. The area was a magnet, too, for European refugees and migrants—some themselves intellectuals or artists.

The Cross attracted actors such as Peter Finch, Ron Randell, Chips Rafferty, Gordon Chater, Dick Bentley and Michael Pate; and artists such as Donald Friend, William Dobell, Sali Herman, Russell Drysdale, Robert Klippel, Emile Mercier and Martin Sharp. There were the poets Kenneth Slessor, Christopher Brennan, Mary Gilmore, Judith Wright, Douglas Stewart and Dorothy Hewitt; writers 'Steele Rudd', Katharine Susannah Pritchard, Dymphna Cusack, Charmion Clift, George Johnston and Frank Clune; publisher Sydney Ure Smith; and musicians Yehudi and Hepzibah Menuhin and Isador Goodman. There was a crowned Queen of Bohemia (writer Dulcie Deamer); an artistic witch (Rosaleen Norton); and homeless Bea Miles, who spouted Shakespeare on demand. Once she told a taxi driver to take her to Perth. He did, and Bea paid in cash.

While the rest of Australia tucked itself quietly into bed at night, Kings Cross never did. Earnest intellectuals, artists, drop-outs and hangers-on congregated nightly in cafes, galleries and pubs; or in dozens of tiny, smoke-filled flats. It was reputedly the most crowded square mile on Earth—Australia's Montmartre, Greenwich Village and Soho—an apprenticeship here was one of the essential badges of artistic courage.

But the rents went up and the times, they were a'changing. Bohemia drowned in a tide of Vietnam War R&R spending and sleaze, tourism, sex shows, drugs, real estate escalation, mega-dollar redevelopments and economic rationalism. The artists became respectable or speech-writers, and the intellectuals became managers or stockbrokers—Sydney's Bohemia went, and nothing came to replace it.

Elizabeth Bay House—regal once more after doing time as a boarding house for Bohemia.

houses popular with young artists and writers, until the World War II navy takeover of the area. Take the opportunity to read the historical plaques by the gate.

Now retrace your steps along Wylde Street, but continue past Grantham Street and beyond the curve where Wylde becomes Macleay Street. McDonald Street, Challis Avenue and Rockwall Crescent have fine surviving terraces. The elegant Regency simplicity of architect John Verge's **'Rockwall'** ⑧, built between 1830 and 1837 for civil engineer John Busby, stands in Rockwall Crescent. Busby engineered Sydney's first water supply tunnel (see feature box, page 29).

Back on Macleay, retrace your steps 100 metres or so and, just before Challis Avenue, cross to a small laneway next to number 18 Macleay Street (signposted 'Elizabeth Bay House'). This short lane emerges into the totally different world of Elizabeth Bay, beginning with architecturally varied Billyard Avenue.

The main attraction in this area is on Onslow Avenue, off Billyard to the right. An elegant survivor, **Elizabeth Bay House** ⑨, sits amidst surrounding high-rise on a pocket of land barely big enough to stop it spilling into the roadway. The little Arthur McElhone Reserve at the front offers only a hint of the house's original 22-hectare botanical garden setting. The interior of Elizabeth Bay House, now a Historic Houses Trust property, features a central staircase curving up towards an arcaded gallery under a great oval-shaped dome. The Colonial Regency-style house, partly designed by architect John Verge, was built between 1835 and 1839 for the Colonial Secretary,

Alexander Macleay (1767–1848). Apart from his government duties—rewarded by the Elizabeth Bay grant in 1826—Macleay was an exceptional natural historian, and his garden and entomological collection gained international repute. The family scientific tradition continued, culminating in the establishment of the Macleay Museum at Sydney University. The house's gardens progressively shrank under development until the last section disappeared in 1927. From 1941 until its 1970s restoration, the house was divided into flats. Artist Donald Friend watched the Japanese submarine raid in 1942 from the rooftop, and decided then and there to join the army.

From the reserve, look down to number 28 Billyard Avenue with its rooftop pond—one of its six apartments sold for $7 million in late 1998. Take the steps down into Onslow Avenue and head east towards Ithaca Road where glimpses through wrought-iron grilles in Spanish Mission walls reveal a movie set of fountains, paved courtyards and loggia, overtopped by a mango tree. The sense of Hollywood is no accident: the style was popularised by the movies—this house even had its own basement cinema. The metal plaques, bearing the unlikely name **'Boomerang'** ⑩, reflect the trademark of J. Albert and Sons, music publishers, and the house—probably Australia's first in Spanish Mission style—was designed in 1926 by Neville Hampson for the proprietor, Frank Albert (1874–1962). Turn left into Ithaca Road and cross to waterfront Beare Park, a pleasant place for a pause and water views. The garden and terraced lawns of theatrical entrepreneur

J. C. Williamson's home, 'Tudor'—a house almost legendary for its lavish entertainments—once reached the water here. Return to Ithaca Road and follow it up to Elizabeth Bay Road. 'Ithaca Gardens' apartments, near the intersection, is a 1957 adornment to the area by architect Harry Seidler.

Some 100 metres to the left, Elizabeth Bay Road suddenly opens into the wonderful space of Macleay Reserve, surrounded by buildings that could serve as the Australian museum of multiple occupancy. There is Federation 'Keudeau' to the left; Victorian Gothic 'Aringa' to the right; Anglo-Dutch 'Cheddington' at number 63, Victorian Italianate at numbers 86–88, and Victorian Second Empire in the form of 'Ashton', number 102, with its minuscule widow's walk. The interwar period is represented by the Art Deco Skyscraper Gothic of 'Adereham Hall' at number 71 (once nicknamed 'Gotham City'), the Functionalist/P&O style 'Ashdown' at number 96, the Mediterranean 'Beverley Hall' down tiny Elizabeth Bay Crescent, and the Spanish Mission styles at 'Beuna Vista'(also down Elizabeth Bay Crescent) and at number 81 Elizabeth Bay Road. There are also modern, international style blocks, the best being 'Toft Monks' (number 95) and 'International Lodge' (number 100); and at the far end are the visually satisfying organic curves of the late 20th-century modern tower of 'Deepdene' (number 110).

Two earlier mansions, both stone Regency style, survive. Number 97 is 'Tresco', designed and built as his own home by architect Colonel Thomas Rowe. Number 93, complete with stables, is **'Kincoppal'**, designed by John Sharkey in 1870 for merchant John Hughes. The wealthy Hughes left the house to the French Order of the Sacred Heart who established Kincoppal school here. In 1970 the school moved to the Convent above Rose Bay (see Walk 5, page 38) and these grounds were later redeveloped with home units.

Retrace your steps along Elizabeth Bay Road, following it around past where it meets Greenknowe Avenue. Looming on the right—dramatised by its elevated position—is Emil Sodersten's brick deco apartments, **'Birtley Towers'**, in 1934 the largest block of flats in Australia. Take Ward Avenue past the back of Fitzroy Gardens to Roslyn Street and turn uphill to Darlinghurst Road. This is the Cross full on—cosmopolitan, bustling, ambient and touristy—with nightclubs, drugs, prostitution, sex-shops and corruption. Tourists in their thousands stay in everything from five-star hotels to backpacker hostels, and locals survive around the fringes despite high rents. Restaurants mingle with strip joints and souvenir shops, everything jostling along in a suburb still offering more opportunities to entertain and offend than anywhere else in Sydney.

Kings Cross station, and the end of the walk, is along Darlinghurst Road to the left.

Walk 2

A Touch of Class

Darling Point

Features
Historic houses and religious buildings • waterfront views and parks • historic personalities.

Distance
Approx. 4km return.

Time
2 hours.

Difficulty
Easy to moderate • some steps • strollers OK • wheelchairs generally not.

Access
Buses and rail (Edgecliff railway station and interchange) • street parking.
UBD: Map 4 Q11
Gregory's: Map 13 K11.

Facilities
Toilets at McKell Park • picnic spots at McKell Park and Yarranabbe Park.

The closest seriously wealthy suburb to the city, Darling Point is a sometimes uncomfortable mix of brashly oversized apartment blocks and dignified old world mansions watching their neighbours disdainfully from deep gardens. But with its serene atmosphere and wonderful waterfrontages, the Point offers opportunities for elegant exploration.

Additional Reading
Jill Buckland *Mort's Cottage: Impressions of Sydney People and Their Times, 1838–1988*, Kangaroo Press, 1988.
Dinah Dysart & Helen Proudfoot (eds) *Lindesay: a biography of the house*, National Trust, 1984.

Background: St Marks of Darling Point.

From almost day one of its settlement by Europeans, Darling Point had class. Named after Governor Darling's wife, it was subdivided into very large blocks from 1833 to 1835, and the first houses were corners of transplanted English elegance amidst thick native bushland. In the 1840s an early resident, Sir Thomas Mitchell, was robbed of his money and boots on the way home. The locals installed their own watchman after that incident. The intrusive apartment blocks of the 1960s, however, could not be kept out, but enough elegance and great houses survive to show that Darling Point still has class—even if today it is somewhat composite.

The walk begins at the top of Ocean Avenue, across New South Head Road from Edgecliff railway station. About 300 metres down Ocean Avenue turn left into Greenoaks Avenue. Looming above the street's English Arts and Crafts style houses is Darling Point's largest house, **'Bishopscourt'** **❶**, since 1911 the official home of the Anglican Archbishop of Sydney. The Gothic look, enhanced by appropriate gardens, was a popular style amongst the mid-19th-century establishment. Originally called 'Greenoaks', this extravagant house was begun in the mid-1840s, when Lancashire-born Thomas Sutcliffe Mort (1816–78) commissioned it from architect John Frederick Hilly. By 1860 'Greenoaks' had been further expanded by architect Edmund Blacket. Mort, a Sydney auctioneer, merchant, and wool and agricultural broker, expanded his business and public spirited interests to include shipbuilding (Mort's Dock), engineering, railways, agriculture (Goldsborough Mort), minerals, insurance and shipping. He also pioneered the commercial use of refrigeration. A collector of artworks and antiques, Mort established a museum at 'Greenoaks' which, together with the garden, was open to the public. The Anglican Archbishop moved here from Randwick in 1911 (see Walk 10, page 71) and, as the new 'Bishopscourt', the house was enlarged again in the 1920s by architect Leslie Wilkinson (see Walk 5, page 38).

Continue uphill. The houses here are on a part of the 'Greenoaks' garden subdivided in 1910. Note the statue of 'The Dying Gladiator', a relic of the former garden, now in the front garden of number 2D. Enter tree-lined Darling Point Road near the beautifully proportioned Gothic-style **St Mark's church** **❷**. Mort gave the land for the church and Edmund Blacket was commissioned to design it. After some frustration, Blacket won the parishioners over with a sketch based on a thirteenth-century church in Horncastle, Lincolnshire. The antipodean version was built between 1848 and 1864 of Pyrmont sandstone, its soaring spire added in 1870. The Rectory, next door, designed at the same time by Blacket, is also in the Gothic style, providing a pleasing unity.

Darling Point Road shows plenty of signs of its former elegance but also plenty of evidence of the 'flat-out' of the 1960s and since. Across from the church are two attractive houses. At 9 Loftus Road, 'St Canice's' (built in the 1860s for Edward Butler) has become Jean Calvin Hospital; while on the corner of Darling Point Road and Annandale Street is red brick **'Cloncorrick'** **❸**, a distinctive J. Horbury Hunt (see Walk 5, page 38) design, built in 1884 for George Simpson, Attorney-General from 1885 to 1894.

Back on the church side at numbers 69–73 Darling Point Road are two delightful Victorian Filigree pairs with their twin pyramid roofs in Second Empire Style. Turn from Darling Point Road into Marathon Road, then cross into lane-like Mount Adelaide Street, continuing over Eastbourne Road and up to a gateway. 'Mount Adelaide', the home of another Mort, Thomas's brother Henry, once stood here. After Ascham School used it for a time, the house was demolished and replaced in 1912 by the Art Nouveau **'Babsworth House'** 4, the Sydney home of Sir Samuel Hordern (1876–1956) of the Anthony Hordern's merchandising family. Socialite, enthusiastic stockbreeder and racehorse owner, Hordern died here in 1956 and the house eventually became a hospice run by the Sisters of Charity, part of St Vincent's Hospital. Much of its garden has been redeveloped but a short foray through the gates offers a view of the house.

Retrace your steps along Mount Adelaide Street, turn right at Eastbourne and then right into Darling Point Road again. As you follow the road down towards the harbour, only hints of former houses remain—in stone fences or apartment block names. Finally, on the left, the lawns and gardens of **'Swifts'** 5 emerge—but more about this magnificent property later.

Opposite 'Swifts', a series of smaller, almost identical, late-Victorian duplexes begin, giving way further on to individual houses. Enter narrow Carthona Avenue with its stone gateposts. This street is so enclosed it feels eerie, especially with the wash of unseen waves heard as you pass behind 'Lindesay' and the slate roofs and slightly Dutch touches of 'Beach Manor'. At the end of the avenue a glimpse of **'Carthona'** 6 is finally afforded.

Glimpses are about all that can be gained, except from the water, of this Anglo-Scottish Gothic manor house with its creeper, stone battlements, parapets, medieval chimneys and lancet windows. One of the first homes on the point, 'Carthona' was built in 1844 by Major Sir Thomas Mitchell (1792–1855), the distinguished soldier-surveyor and Surveyor-General of New South Wales. Mitchell's explorations and road building (such as the pass at the western end of the Blue Mountains road) contributed to the development of the interiors of New South Wales and Victoria. He sited 'Carthona' (a Spanish word for 'meeting of the waters') where two freshwater streams joined, selecting the house design from a British pattern book, and carving some of the ornamental stonework himself. Competent but testy and vindictive, Mitchell was wounded in 1851 in a duel in Centennial Park with Stuart Donaldson, later first Premier of New South Wales. A 20th-century owner of 'Carthona' was Philip Bushell, an importer and retailer of tea and coffee.

Back at Darling Point Road, the elegant attached villa **'Cintra'** 7 at number 155 was the town house, for most of her adult life, of Dorothea Mackellar (1885–1968), author of what is arguably Australia's national poem, 'My Country' (see Walks 3 and 9). Raised in nearby Point Piper, she moved to 'Cintra' in the 1930s, dividing

Darling Point ☼ 21

Walk 2 Key

- **S** Start
- **1** 'Bishopscourt'
- **2** St Marks church
- **3** 'Cloncorrick'
- **4** 'Babsworth House'
- **5** 'Swifts'
- **6** 'Carthona'
- **7** 'Cintra'
- **8** 'Lindsay'
- **9** McKell Park/'Canonbury' site
- **10** 'Craigend'
- **11** 'The Stables'
- **12** HMAS *Rushcutter* buildings

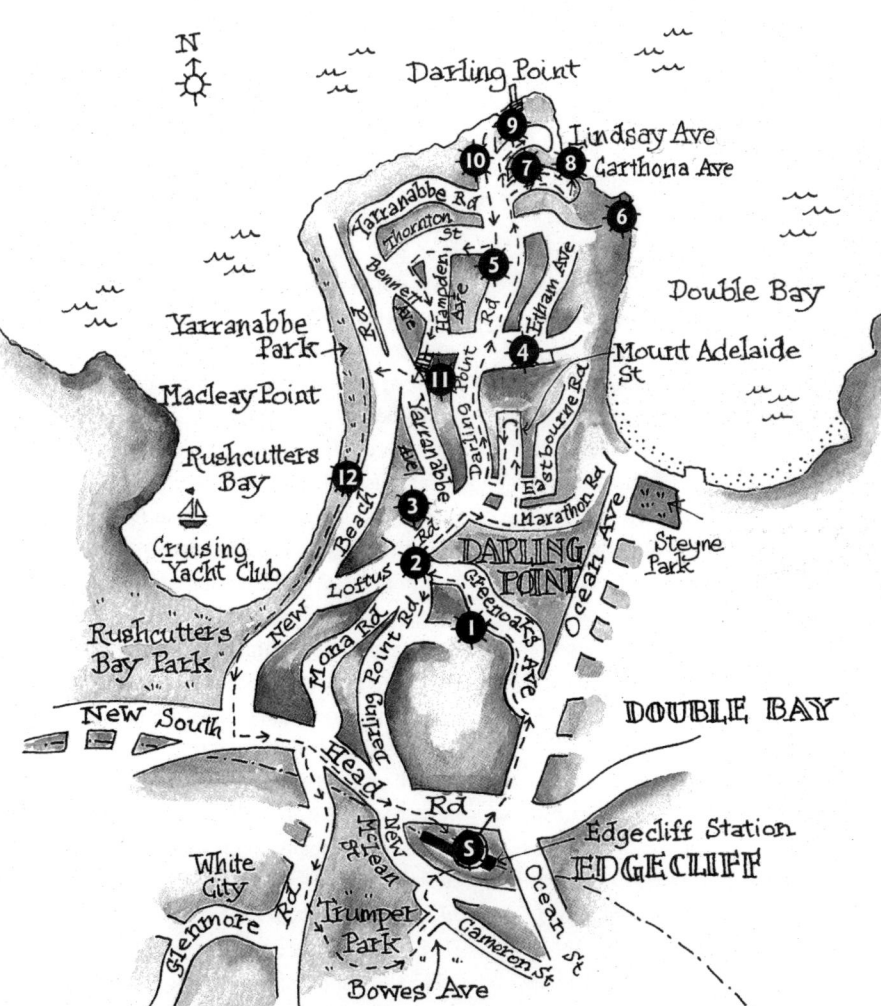

her time between here and her Pittwater retreat. A little way downhill, turn into Lindsay Avenue, passing a serene, if improbable, modern Japanese house, to 'Lindesay' and 'Glanworth'. The latter, with its powerful columns, looks more contemporary than it is, having been built in 1852, although it has been much modified since. Earlier still is **'Lindesay'** 8, the first significant house to be built on Darling Point and one of the earliest Gothic houses in Australia. Its architect, Edward Hallen, borrowed heavily from English style books. Named after Colonel Sir Patrick Lindesay (1778–1839), who was acting Governor in 1831, it was built around 1834 for Colonial Treasurer Campbell Drummond Riddell. Sir Thomas Mitchell resided here whilst 'Carthona' was under construction. It was presented by its last private owner to the National Trust of New South Wales in 1963, and is occasionally open to the public.

Open the garden gate on the low side of the street to step down a short flight of steps into **McKell Park** 9, named for Sir William McKell (1891–1985). A boilermaker who became a barrister, then New South Wales's wartime Labor Premier and, finally, Governor-General, Bill McKell lived his last years as a Double Bay resident. This park is clearly the lovely garden of a fine house. Garden beds edge the lawns, trees frame harbour views, servants' quarters await the call near the main gate, and more steps lead to the water's edge. All that is missing is the house, although its foundations have been integrated into the garden, adding a rustic, romantic touch. At several points plaques tell the story of the houses on the site between 1841 and 1983, principally 'Canonbury', home of Harry Rickards (1847–1911). Rickards, a cockney music hall comedian, came to Sydney in 1871, and in the 1890s established the enormously popular variety and vaudeville theatre The Tivoli. Visit the park's waterfront with its public wharf, remnants of an old stone boathouse and bathing house. Clarke Island sits tantalisingly offshore and, closer to the bridge, Garden Island Naval Base protrudes into the harbour, showing the extent of the infill that ended its island status (see Walk 1, page 11). Walk around the waterfront towards Double Bay where a peep around the end barrier is rewarded with another glimpse of the elusive 'Carthona'.

Return to Darling Point Road via the main park gates. **'Craigend'** 10, the waterfront house opposite McKell Park's main gates, was built in 1935 for shipping and stevedoring magnate James Patrick (1880–1945). Its curious design combination reflects the owner's travels, with Moorish dome and interior details (the dome was added in 1938), Art Deco styling and a Japanese garden. In Patrick's time the house was packed with souvenirs and trophies of exotic travel and hunting, along with novel gadgets including a bookcase in the billiard room that, at the press of a button, slid open to reveal a bar. 'Craigend' served as home for US consul-generals from 1948 to 1988.

Back up the hill a little way, turn right into Thornton Street, where a view of 'Swifts' soon opens up on your left. Designed by G. A. Morrell in the Victorian Tudor style for brewer Robert Lucas Tooth (1821–93), it was built between 1876 and 1882 and named after the Kent estate of

Swamp Stories

The Rushcutters Bay swamps once extended well beyond where New South Head Road is today. In 1788, two convicts cutting rushes there became the first settlers killed by Aborigines. Governor Phillip's enquiries revealed the killings were in retaliation for offences against Aboriginal people and there were no reprisals, but the illusion of peaceful co-existence was gone.

The construction of a bridge across the swamps in the 1830s made Darling Point accessible to the privileged. Eventually the swamps were filled in and mostly replaced by Chinese market gardens. These gave way between 1913 and 1917 to an elaborate amusement park, 'White City', which featured white domes and cupolas above a 'city' of canals, lakes, fountains and a Japanese village, and offered amusements such as roller-skating, rides and illusions. It was replaced by another White City in 1921—the famous courts of the New South Wales Lawn Tennis Association. Inevitably, redevelopment is about to change the area again.

Nearby, a wooden boxing stadium was built in 1908, becoming Sydney's major boxing venue. One of the earliest attractions was Les Darcy, and one of the last, Jimmy Curruthers. From 1956, the stadium also became a music performance venue, and artists such as Frank Sinatra, Sammy Davis Jnr, Johnny O'Keefe, Bob Dylan and The Beatles performed there before the stadium was finally demolished in 1969.

The old swamp also extended right back to Trumper Park, with its Edwardian village oval. Beyond the oval, Trumper Park's regenerated bushland is worth exploring.

The masts of the Cruising Yacht Club of Australia, which runs the Sydney to Hobart Yacht Race, point above Rushcutters Bay to the heights of Darling Point.

the Lucas Tooth family. Tooth wanted to emulate Sydney's Government House, and its 42 rooms included a ballroom larger than the Governor's. In 1901 'Swifts' was purchased by another brewer, Edmond Resch (1847–1923), whose son left it to the Catholic Church for an Archbishop's residence. Consequently, for most of this century both of Sydney's Archbishops resided in Darling Point. The house and grounds were placed under a permanent conservation order in 1984, the Church managing to sell it for $9 million to a private owner in 1986. It was extensively restored in the late 1990s.

Near Thornton Street's junction with Bennett Avenue, elegant apartments such as 'Stratford Hall' survive, but the Hordern family's 'Retford Hall' and 'Hopewood' have been replaced by apartment blocks which retain their names. However, on the corner of Bennett Avenue, 'Callooa' (number 5) remains, a superb many-gabled Gothic mansion built in the 1850s. Follow Bennett Avenue along and turn right into Hampden Avenue. Near the end are two Victorian neighbours, the chunky Second Empire style 'Goomerah' (number 4) dominating the scaled-down Italianate villa at number 2. Ahead, where the footpath ends, steps drop to Yarranabbe Road at **'The Stables' ⓫** (number 28) which, despite the name, is a delightful residence for bipeds.

Zigzag down to New Beach Road and Yarranabbe Park, a reclaimed waterfrontage running almost the full length of Rushcutters Bay (see feature box, page 23) and being developed as the Sailing Shore Base for the 2000 Olympics. Follow New Beach Road back past some buildings formerly part of **HMAS Rushcutter** ⓬, once the oldest Royal Australian Navy base, to Rushcutters Bay Park. The Cruising Yacht Club of Australia dominates the area, the masts of expensive boats filling the Bay. The Sydney–Hobart Yacht Race begins here each Boxing Day.

Back at New South Head Road, if you've had enough walking, turn uphill to the left and walk back and across the road to Edgecliff Station, where the walk began.

However, if there's still a little energy and time available, cross over towards, the Eastern Suburbs Railway viaduct and turn into Glenmore Road. Trumper Park, with its quaint cricket oval, soon appears. Originally called Hampden Park, it was renamed after the Paddington cricketing sensation, Victor Trumper (1877–1915), the greatest Australian batsman before Bradman. He scored 16,929 runs in first class cricket, including 2750 against England in the 1902 test series. In one first grade match he made 50 runs in less than six minutes. Trumper dies, aged 38, of Bright's Disease.

Beyond the oval, Trumper Park's hillside is a rare oasis in this area, with huge fig trees, regenerated bushland, pond, tennis courts and views.

From the area above the back of the oval, tiny Bowes Avenue leads into terraces at Cameron Street, where a left turn brings you almost immediately to the back of the Edgecliff Station complex.

Walk 3

Arsenals & Old Lace

Paddington

From a brewery, a scattering of fine houses, a cluster of pubs and brothels about an army barracks in the sandhills and, later, a despised slum, Paddington has developed into one of Sydney's jewels—a quintessentially trendy terrace suburb whose characteristic ironwork has entered the language as 'Paddington lace'.

Additional Reading
Woollahra Heritage Proms: hands-on history walking tours in the Woollahra area, Woollahara History and Heritage Society, 1996

Background: Five Ways and the Royal Hotel epitomise the Paddington look and lifestyle.

Features
Diverse domestic architecture, extensive terraces • galleries, antique shops • Georgian military barracks.

Distance
Approx. 5½ km return.

Time
3 hours.

Difficulty
Easy • some steps; strollers OK • mostly wheelchair accessible.

Access
Oxford Street buses; street parking (mostly restricted).
UBD: Map 4 F16
Gregory's: Map 13 A16.

Facilities
No public toilets or picnic spots en route; plenty of pubs, cafes and shops throughout.

26 ❊ Sydney Strolls ❊ Eastern Suburbs

Walk 3 Key

- **S** Start
- **1** Town Hall
- **2** 'Juniper Hall'
- **3** Georgian terraces
- **4** 'Olive Bank Villa'
- **5** Part of 'Englehurst'
- **6** Original site of Royal Hospital for Women
- **7** Workers' cottages
- **8** The Scottish Hospital
- **9** Royal Hotel
- **10** 'Warwick'
- **11** Former Woollahra Congregational church
- **12** St Francis of Assisi church
- **13** 'Runnymede'
- **14** Police Station/ Courthouse

Paddington's name, and much of its Victorian and Edwardian architectural style, is borrowed from London. Had Sydney's post-World War II planners had their way, Paddington's then 'run-down slums' would have been blitzed like many of their London counterparts and replaced by a monolithic landscape of flats. Today's spruced up, fashionable ranks of terraces with their suggestion of intellectual and arty lifestyles, do not look much like the neglected, low-rent rows of the 1940s. Their survival and revival came through an attitudinal change towards Victorian architecture and city living, led firstly by the postwar European migrants, and taken up by the conservation-minded Paddington Society.

The walk begins in Oxford Street at the 1885 Post Office, opposite the 1891 **Town Hall** ❶. Both buildings represent Paddington at its Victorian peak around 1890, when steam trams puffed along bustling Oxford Street and Paddington was New South Wales's third wealthiest municipality. In the preceding 20 years Paddington had exploded in size, with almost 4000 houses, mostly terraces, built and the population increasing seven-fold to 18 000. The municipality gave itself a suitably grand Classical Revival style Town Hall, designed by local architect J. E. Kemp with a clock tower 32.5 metres high. Within two more decades, however, terraced Paddington had begun a slide to slum status as fashionable home-makers moved to new, more distant, detached-dwelling suburbs. In the course of this decline even the municipality disappeared, annexed by the City of Sydney in 1949 and remaining within it until 1967 when most of the suburb was added to Woollahra Municipality.

A short walk east towards the shops brings you to one of the oldest and most significant buildings in Paddington, **'Juniper Hall'** ❷. A number of such villas on large estates developed here, later to be subdivided into the present terraced streets. 'Juniper Hall' is probably the oldest surviving villa in Australia, its name originating from the berry used to make gin. 'Robert the Large' Cooper, a London publican transported to Sydney for smuggling, had, with two partners, established a successful distillery above Rushcutters Bay in 1818. Larger than life in most matters, Cooper promised his third wife, Sarah (mother of 14 of his 28 children), the finest house in Sydney—a promise he kept here in 1824. Renamed 'Ormond House' by a later owner, Judge Kinchella, it eventually became institutions and flats, disappearing behind a row of shops, before its restoration by the National Trust in 1984. It is now privately leased.

Turn right into Underwood Street, following it around past some uninspiring flats to Bennetts Grove Avenue. Thomas Underwood was one of Cooper's distillery partners and the row of single-storey **Georgian terraces** ❸ on the corner is amongst Paddington's earliest, built on his estate in the 1840s to accommodate the families of officers at Victoria Barracks. Underwood named his 100-acre (41-hectare) subdivision 'Paddington'. Continue up Underwood Street and turn left into Union Street, noting stone number 17, and then numbers 36–46, a beautiful row of single-storey Gothic terraces with elaborate and decorative timberwork.

From Union, turn into Stafford Street, where a full range of terrace styles is presented—terraces like villas; Gothic semis with gingerbread gables and Italianate decoration; high-set Federation terraces; and Victorian boom-style 'wedding-cake' filigree terraces. A competition in classical ornateness seems to have occurred, with fine wrought-iron (mostly Sydney-made), elaborate plasterwork, classical adornments like lions and urns, and house names reflecting Greek and Roman literature and mythology. At the end of Stafford, turn right down Heeley Street past fine pre-1890s terraces to **'Olive Bank Villa'** 4, now a kindergarten on the corner of Olive Street. A colonial-style house completed in 1869, for John Begg, it was the last built of the Paddington mansions. Follow Olive Street to Ormond Street, turning uphill amidst impressive terraces. Between the flats at 56A and 56B Ormond Street notice, amongst 1920s apartments, the odd remnant of another early mansion, **'Englehurst'** 5, designed in 1835 by John Verge for Frederick Hely, Supervisor of Convicts.

Back on Oxford Street, turn downhill towards the city. The Paddington Green development between Young and Brodie streets replaces the **Royal Hospital for Women** 6, where many Sydneysiders were born between 1904 and 1997. The opposite side of Oxford Street is dominated by the impressive wall of Victoria Barracks (see feature box, page 29), which brought the first wave of intense settlement to the area from the 1840s. The Paddington Green Hotel had its origins as the c1855 Green Gate Hotel, one of many soldiers' pubs. Opposite the Victoria Barracks entrance, turn into Shadforth Street and enter the old village of Paddington, dating back to the establishment of the barracks. Beyond it in the 1850s, most of what is now Paddington was still rocky hillsides, scrub or sandhills. Many of the stone and sandstock brick cottages and terraces crammed into these little streets housed the workers, craftsmen, shopkeepers, blacksmiths, grog-shops and prostitutes never far from any barracks. Many were built by the same British contractors and craftsmen who built the Barracks. From Shadforth turn left into Gipps Street, noting the former corner store with its fading old advertising—corner shops were once the lifeblood of the inner city, averaging one to every 45 houses. Follow Gipps Street's interesting cottages to Prospect Street. The 1840s **corner cottages** 7 (numbers 1 and 3 Prospect) are amongst the oldest left in Paddington, even retaining shingled tiles under their iron roofs. Take a short diversion past the cottages dotted along Prospect and Spring streets.

Return to Gipps Street and, at Glenmore Road, turn right at the decorative Rose and Crown Hotel (1890). Glenmore Road began as a meandering cart-track to the former Glenmore Distillery, but now belongs to gentrified Paddington with bookshops and, especially, galleries—of which the suburb has many. The shops and homes of Glenmore Road had substance and style from the beginning, with fine sandstone terraces and occasional villas, such as numbers 41–43.

After a fair walk down Glenmore turn left at Brown Street, crossing the old tramway passage at the corner. The 1910

The Barracks

Sydney's first barracks were at Wynyard Square. Their relocation to Paddington in 1848 caused complaints from soldiers about being consigned to an isolated site far from town. The 11.7-hectare site had been chosen because it had bore water, suitable building stone on site and was on the presumed advance line an attacker from the east might use. The only attack actually met was by flying sand from the adjacent sandhills.

Designed in Georgian Regency style by Lieutenant-Colonel George Barney, convict labourers, contractors and army engineers began work in 1841. Completed by 1849, the barracks were occupied by five different British regiments until British troops were withdrawn from New South Wales in 1870. The site was not fully occupied again until the Boer War, and Paddington worthies complained resentfully that the barracks were an eyesore occupying valuable land. After Federation, the barracks were transferred to the Commonwealth and in both world wars formed army administrative headquarters. Since then they have been HQ 2nd Military District and Land HQ.

The barracks sit atop a section of Busby's Bore, a convict-built tunnel which provided Sydney's main water supply from 1837 to 1859, bringing water from the Centennial Park area to Hyde Park. The bore, designed by engineer John Busby (see Walk 1), included 28 shafts and wells—two within the barracks area, the deepest of which (more than 25 metres) has been restored. It is part of a barracks guided tour at 10 a.m. on Thursdays, as is the Barracks museum, which is also open on Sundays.

Military architecture at its most elegant—the main barracks block at Victoria Barracks.

Federation-style terraces beyond MacDonald Street are amongst the last built in Paddington before inner-city living and attached housing began to lose their appeal. The outbreak of Bubonic Plague in Sydney in 1900 had accentuated the view that terraces were crowded and disease-prone, and garden suburbs and single bungalows came into vogue (see Walk 11, page 78).

Turn right into Cooper Street at the **Scottish Hospital** 8. 'The Terraces', Judge Kinchella's mansion around which the hospital developed, survives here along with century-old trees and terraces. A later owner, surgeon Sir Alexander MacCormick, gave it to the Presbyterian Church for a hospital in 1926. The poet Dorothea Mackellar (see Walks 2 and 9) died here in 1968. Cooper Street continues along with a streetscape varying from Victorian villas to bad 1960s. Note the postmodern number 8A with its circular opening and peek-a-boo tree above the entrance, suggesting something enticing behind the unobtrusive exterior. This prize-winning house, designed by architect Ken Woolley in 1980 as his own home, grows towards the city on a steep block, presenting an angled three-storey facade to the view. Opposite numbers 6–8, take the very narrow passageway between houses which climbs back to meandering Glenmore Road.

Turn left and the village crossroads of Five Ways is directly ahead. This is classic Paddington, a charming mixture of shops and terraces, dominated by the 1888 grand Classical-style **Royal Hotel** 9. There are harbour glimpses downhill as you cross to continue briefly along Glenmore Road past brick St George's church (1890s) before turning right into Gurner Street with its attractive houses. Beyond the intersection with Cambridge and Norfolk Streets, the village green-like bus-stop area is another survival of the tramline which once ran through here to North Bondi, paralleling the Oxford Street line which travelled via Bondi Junction to Bondi and the other eastern beaches. Turn uphill into Norfolk Street to where fine terraces all but form an impressive urban square. Typically, Paddington terraces were built by small owner–speculators, who each bought enough land for perhaps half-a-dozen attached houses. They built the first house and lived in it, added another and as it was rented, added more until the terrace was completed. It was this piecemeal, individualistic development which accounts for the infinite variety in what at first glance may seem like uniform rows of terraces.

Norfolk Street now turns left, narrows into a short lane and ends at a short flight of steps beside some handsome Gothic villas above steep Cascade Street. There are fine views and an interesting castellated corner house, **'Warwick'** 10, opposite. Here the Glenmore Falls once cascaded over rocks, bringing a clear stream of water down to Cooper and partners' Glenmore Distillery in the valley below. A later owner of the distillery plant, James Begg, diverted the stream and created Cascade Street as part of a subdivision. Take the steps down into this street of fine rising terraces and cross into elegant, tree-lined Windsor Street, following it to Elizabeth Street. Almost inevitably, on the Elizabeth–Windsor intersection, stands the Windsor Castle hotel.

At Elizabeth Street turn uphill and then left into Paddington Street. This handsome, tree-lined thoroughfare brings together quite a variety of dwellings and styles—and more galleries. Rudy Komon set up Paddington's very first gallery at the Jersey Road corner in 1958. Turn left at Jersey Road and walk to the former **Woollahra Congregational church** ⓫. Designed by architect Benjamin Backhouse in 1877, after a 1989 fire it remained a romantic ruin for years until adaptation to housing was begun in 1998.

Turn right into busy Moncur Street. Don't miss the block of flats on the Woollahra side of the road at numbers 81–83 Moncur—they were once better known as 'No. 96' in the 1970s TV soapie of that name. Around the Queen Street intersection the level of activity and fashion increases. This has been a fashionable area for some time and much wealth and influence is tucked away in these leafy streets, even though some former mansions have gone. At the intersection itself, most corners belong to a different era with a Federation Post Office (1904), Victorian shops and a deco pub. This area was transformed in the 1960s and 1970s, resident action restraining overmuch modernisation which threatened its charm and vitality.

After exploring the coffee, book and food shops of the area, turn right down Queen Street towards Oxford Street, past Sydney's most concentrated array of fine art, antique and antiquity shops and galleries. Opposite the medical centre, Hall's Lane slips away to the right. Follow it through to the Jersey Road–Rush Street junction.

Jersey Road offers a final touch of restrained elegance before the bustle of Oxford Street where the Romanesque rose window of **St Francis of Assisi church** ⓬ (1890–1917) floats tantalisingly in the distance. Apart from the familiar terraces, numbers 47–41 are a foretaste of the Jersey Road mansions. Number 48, now crowded in by the street, is inviting, but it is numbers 23–17 that take the prize. The first, **'Runnymede'** ⓭ (number 23) retains its wonderful Georgian elegance in its garden setting. Opposite the last, number 17 ('Westbourne', from 1868), stands the 1888 Victorian Classical **Police Station–Courthouse** ⓮, designed by James Barnet.

The end of the walk is 500 metres away along an Oxford Street heavily booby-trapped with enticing shops and cafes. This shopping centre was well established by the 1890s and if it is Saturday, the 1877 Uniting church across the road will be hosting the irresistible Paddington Bazaar. It could be a long 500 metres.

Walk 4

Social Climbing

Bondi Junction, Bellevue Hill, Woollahra, Edgecliff

Beginning in the hub of Bondi Junction, this varied and upwardly mobile walk is between railway stations on the once infamous Eastern Suburbs Line. It centres on wooded Cooper Park but branches out into the loftier establishment eyries of Bellevue Hill, Woollahra and Edgecliff.

Additional Reading
Woollahra Heritage Proms: Hands-on History Walking Tours in the Woollahra Area, Woollahara History and Heritage Society, 1996

Background: Looking to Bondi—part of the beautiful view from Bellevue Hill.

Features
Intriguing parkland
• a panoramic view
• diverse architecture
• consulates.

Distance
Approx. 6km.

Time
2–3 hours.

Difficulty
Easy to moderate
• some steps • strollers generally manageable
• wheelchairs generally not.

Access
Bondi Junction rail and buses • parking stations at Bondi Junction, some street parking.
UBD: Map 257 D3
Gregory's: Map 22 H6.

Facilities
Toilets and kiosk at Cooper Park • picnic spots at Cooper and Bellevue parks
• shops at either end of the walk.

Bondi Junction was once called Tea Gardens after a local pub, but its development as a hub for eastern suburbs tram services from the city to Bronte, Waverley, Clovelly, Randwick, Coogee and Bondi changed the area's name to its present one. The crowded shopping centre is most conveniently approached by train or bus. For those arriving this way, Bondi Junction is the last station on the Eastern Suburbs Railway, a long-kicked political football until it was finally opened in 1979. The rail opening deprived political cartoonists of one of their longest-running targets and helped fill the gap made 20 years earlier with the removal of the trams which had until then converged on the Junction.

The walk begins in Grafton Street outside the Bondi Junction station entrance and passes through the commuter car park underneath Syd Einfeld Drive to Rowe Street. Walking in the direction of the harbour, you enter an area of terraces, including some in fine Gothic style at Edgecliff Road. Turn right into Edgecliff Road, with its intermingling of decorator shops and terraces. At leafy Adelaide Street, cast a glance back up to the brick steeple on the very 1940s **Holy Cross church** ❶. From 1874 to 1901 the Adelaide (later Waverley) Brewery was located here utilising a freshwater spring. Now turn down Adelaide Street, where a concrete wall at its end announces Cooper Park. Before descending, take a short diversion to the right into the bowery walk of Adelaide Parade, surely one of the most charming terrace settings in Sydney.

Follow the flight of steps down into Cooper Park. A real Jurassic Park, this woodland valley originated with an extrusion of volcanic magma in the Jurassic period, the central stream running through it indicates the line of the dyke. After the first steps, the track splits into three. Take the middle of the alternative paths but turn right immediately before a bridge over a stone-lined waterfall. From this point an unpaved path descends gently above the tennis courts into a clearing with a charming stone pavilion. Continue around to the right, down over a bridge to the floor of the park valley. Across another bridge, towards the tennis courts, is an **information board** ❷ giving some of the park's history and showing its walking paths. In the late 1920s and 1930s the park was redesigned as a bushland pleasure ground with landscaped walks, rustic features and a mix of native and exotic trees. This varied quality remains.

Cooper Park gained its name from the large Cooper family estate of which it was part from 1827, and about half the present 15-hectare park was donated to Council by Sir William Cooper in 1913 (see feature box, page 36). It doesn't much matter which of the many paths are taken as you climb eastwards up the length of the valley, but the cliff walks on the northern side are the most interesting to explore, with their rainforest vegetation, small waterfalls and bridges. The central paths follow the stream and its artificial ponds and archaic bridges, linking up at frequent intervals with the upper paths on either side. Eventually some substantial steps are reached which climb the open bowl of the park's head to Victoria Road (past some stone columns from Sydney's old Post Office) in Bellevue Hill.

The view is not quite 'belle' yet, so cross Victoria into short Bellevue Park Road. At its end, a round hilltop park reveals the reason for the area's name in a breathtaking 180° sweep of harbour and ocean from Bradleys Head to Bondi. The harbour views include Clifton Gardens, Shark Island, Rose Bay, the Sacred Heart Convent and Manly. The Heads are masked by the rise of Vaucluse and Dover Heights beyond the Royal Sydney Golf Course but, further south, red roofs lead down to North Bondi and the prominent 1889 sewer vent 'chimney' at the Williams Park golf course. Down past Ben Buckler headland lies the blue of Bondi Bay, though the beach itself is hidden behind buildings. Masses of unit blocks absorb the rest of the southern view.

Lachlan Macquarie, Governor of New South Wales between 1810 and 1821 named the area well, and throughout the 19th century, Sydney gentry took Sunday carriage rides out here to picnic. Many of the gentry, such as the Fairfaxes and the Foys, decided to stay on, and the slopes towards the harbour on the left, or across the golf course at Vaucluse, are among Sydney's most expensive suburbs (as a ramble at another time around the streets to the east of Bellevue Road would confirm). Houses here were momentarily a little less expensive after the night of 7 June 1942 when shells fired from the Japanese submarine I24 off Bondi landed on the crest of this hill. Other shells rained down in an arc from Cooper Park to near the Rose Bay Flying Base, the apparent target. Most failed to explode and there were no casualties but enthusiasm for eastern suburbs real estate briefly declined. Ten days earlier a midget submarine launched from the large Japanese submarine I24 had sunk HMAS *Kuttabul* at Garden Island (see Walks 1 and 7) with 19 killed, and three days after that the I24 itself sank an Australian ore carrier, the *Iron Crown*, off Sydney's Heads killing 12 more seamen. No wonder the locals were jumping ship.

Choose from the many alternative paths when retracing your steps back through Cooper Park. Then, from the tennis courts near the western end, follow the grass out to where Manning Road and Edward Street join near a **sandstone motor garage** ❸ from an earlier era.

If time is limited, it is easy to return to Bondi Junction from here. Turn left into Edward Street with its wonderful double-gabled Gothic villas stepping up the hillside, and then across into tree-lined Russell Street and into the tiny amphitheatre of Harbour View Park and up the substantial steps to Magney Street, an elegant continuation of Russell. Edgecliff Road is just ahead and a quick left along it and then a right at Newland Street leads back to Bondi Junction station.

However, the far more interesting alternative is to continue on from Cooper Park to Edgecliff station. In this case, turn right down Manning Road at the old garage and take the first left, Linden Avenue. This is an area of many architectural preferences: Spanish Mission, interwar English, French Provincial, Classical, and affluent. At split-level Wallaroy Road, climb to the higher level for a look back at the tree-filled bowl of Cooper Park, and then head north in the direction of the harbour. Near where the road reunites, take the steps up to the left

Bondi Junction, Bellevue Hill, Woollahra, Edgecliff ☀ 35

Walk 4 Key

- **S** Start
- **1** Holy Cross church
- **2** Cooper Park information board
- **3** Old stone motor garage
- **4** 'Roslyndale'
- **5** 'Hillside Flats'
- **6** 'Rosemont'
- **7** Consulates
- **8** All Saints church

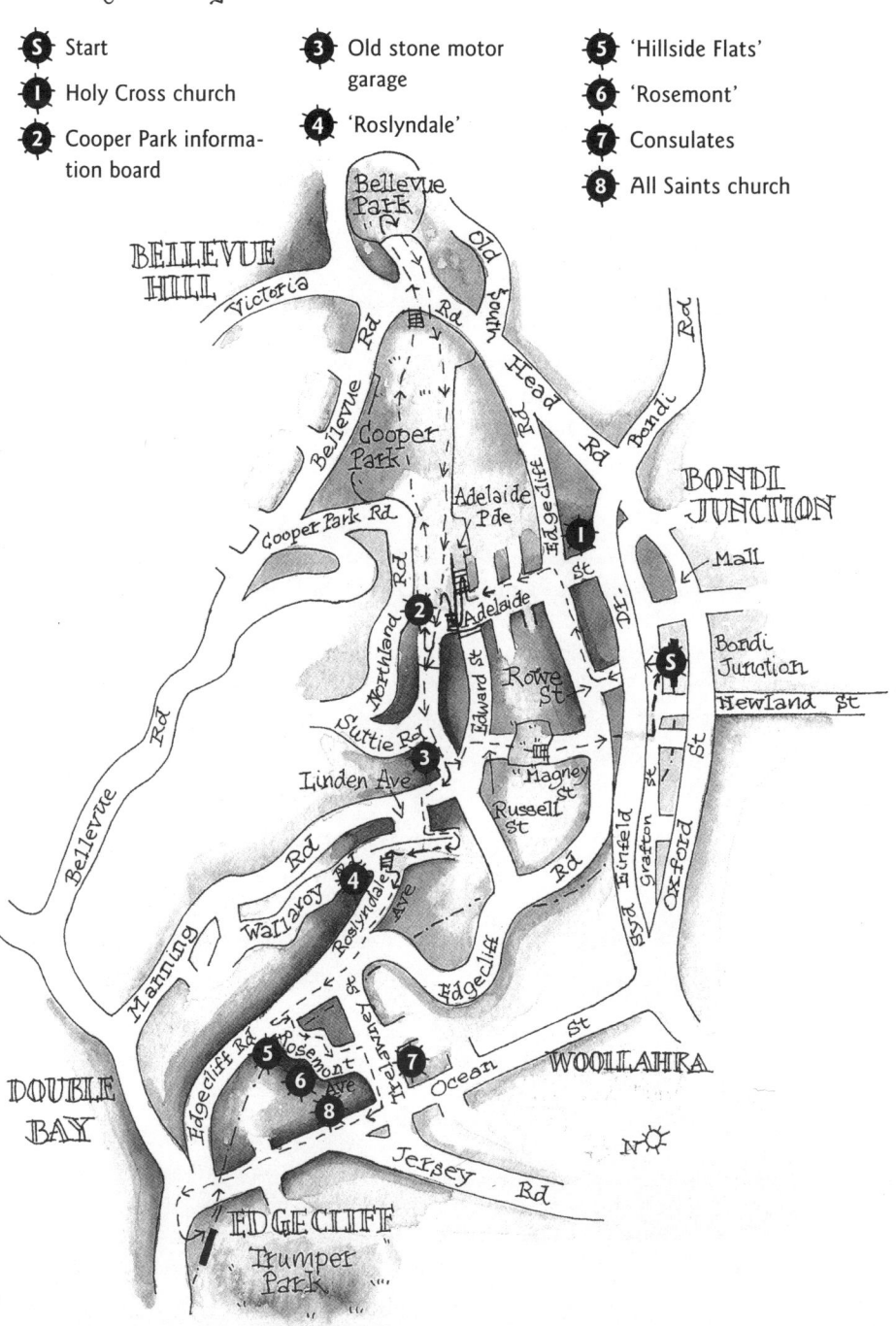

(signposted Roslyndale Avenue) to emerge into a delightful square of modest semis. At the top of the steps is number 38, **'Roslyndale'** ④. Warm in sandstone, adorned by steep gables with elegant and intricate traceried bargeboards, this late 1850s rustic Gothic-style home was designed by Francis Clarke for broker William Lennon. Roslyndale Avenue continues with Mediterranean and Spanish themes on both sides. To the right note number 6, 'Hawthornden', with its fine gates and marvellous setting. It was begun in 1858 by William Lennon.

The Baronet of Woollahra

How appropriate that this municipality—in which a large part of the nation's private wealth, power, social aspiration, diplomatic and commercial representation is concentrated—should once have had its own baron.

Daniel Cooper (1785–1853) was transported as a convict to Australia in 1816 and became one of the colony's most successful merchants. His nephew and namesake, Daniel Cooper (1821–1902), came freely to Australia in 1843. By the time Daniel the younger inherited his uncle's estate a decade later, he was already a wealthy land owner. His Double Bay estate included most of what had been the estate of the flamboyant and extravagant Captain John Piper, who had fallen into financial ruin in 1827. In 1856 Cooper began a great mansion called 'Woollahra House' on the site of Captain Piper's 'Henrietta Villa'. In the same year he became first Speaker of New South Wales's new Legislative Assembly. Knighted in 1857, he resigned in 1860 and returned to England a year later, the great house still not built. Sir Daniel was made the First Baronet of Woollahra in 1863, often working on behalf of, but not returning to, New South Wales. The grand house, completed in 1883 by Cooper's son William, was offered to New South Wales in 1902. The State turned the offer down, the estate was progressively sold and the house was demolished in 1929.

Not quite the Baronial lodge, but Adelaide Parade/'Roslyndale' is a lovely part of the heritage of the former Cooper Estate.

At Edgecliff Road the large Federation house on the Trelawney Street corner, with its elegant wood turning on its levels of verandahs, is hard to miss. Stroll downhill to the right to Rosemont Avenue and a little beyond to admire **'Hillside Flats'** ⑤, the amazing Skyscraper Gothic complex of textured red brick designed by Pitt and Bolot in 1936. Look upwards from both frontages to get its full value, noting especially the pinnacles with their brick flying buttresses.

Meander along serpentine Rosemont Avenue with its lovely trees and large and elegant houses. The house **'Rosemont'** ⑥, built between 1858 and 1859, is now largely hidden by later developments. It was the home from the 1930s to 1958 of merchant and art-lover Sir Charles Lloyd Jones, Chairman of David Jones Ltd. Enter Trelawney Street almost opposite the interesting Wolper Jewish Hospital and turn right to continue uphill past the imposing buildings of some of Sydney's **consulates** —look for Poland, Germany, Yugoslavia and Belgium ⑦. Sydney has more consulates (70 plus) than Canberra has embassies and about a third of them are located in this part of the eastern suburbs.

At Ocean Street, take in the charming street scene on the city side of the road which includes the Georgian-like number 84 and the partially shingled Gothic number 82. There is plenty more elegance back in that direction, but turn right instead, along Ocean Street. Across the road, the facade of the Goethe Institut (the German cultural organisation) stands near where Jersey Road angles in. Don't miss **All Saints church** ⑧ set back up on the rise here on the right. It is a very fine Edmund Blacket design concealing a surprisingly large and noble interior with excellent stained glass windows. First opened in 1876, it was not completed until 1926 and its intended spire was never added. As well as being a Blacket design, there is another link between this church's origins and that of nearby St Mark's at Darling Point (see Walk 2, page 18). Thomas Sutcliffe Mort provided the land and much support for St Mark's, while his brother, Henry Mort, largely financed All Saints. Henry's generosity had several motives. In 1865 Henry's family had been shipwrecked in the Atlantic and rescued after 10 days, so All Saints was an act of thanksgiving. It also provided a living for Henry's son, Henry Wallace Mort who, for 38 years, was the church's first rector.

Beyond All Saints, more recent buildings mingle with wide terraces and slightly tired Victorian villas, including the modest terrace consulate of Portugal. At the bottom of the road, where Ocean Street meets New South Head Road, lies Edgecliff station, which can be accessed from Ocean Street, down a footpath beside the bus ramp to the interchange, or from around the corner in New South Head Road. From here you can catch the train into the city or back one station to Bondi Junction. Buses are available here to various destinations.

Walk 5

Hermitage Heritage

Rose Bay, Nielsen Park, Vaucluse

Features
Magnificent harbour and foreshore scenery • bushland • domestic, school and religious architecture.

Distance
Approx. 5 km • links with Walk 6.

Time
2 hours.

Difficulty
Easy to moderate • many steps and inclines • Nielsen Park OK for strollers and wheelchairs.

Access
New South Head Road buses (Vaucluse) • street parking. UBD: Map 237 N7 Gregory's: Map 348 C7.

Facilities
Toilets, picnic spots at Nielsen Park. No dogs in national park.

Few walks in Sydney begin as spectacularly as this. You stand above Rose Bay with, on one hand, Sydney's ageless harbour twisting and turning below between opposing shorelines towards the arch of the bridge and, on the other hand, the improbable towering of a huge convent seemingly transplanted from medieval France.

Additional Reading
Eric Russell *Woollahra, a History in Pictures*, John Ferguson, 1980.

Background: A fine retreat for a hermit—the 'Hermitage' above Hermit Bay.

The walk follows the Rose Bay foreshore to Nielsen Park, returning through some of Australia's most expensive real estate. Virtually all of this walk takes place on land once part of the 240-hectare Vaucluse estate of the Wentworth family (see Walk 6, page 45). If driving, park down steep Bayview Hill Road and begin this walk at a lower level—catching up on the view at the end. If arriving by bus, begin with the harbour view from the **lookout** ❶ at the junction of Bayview Hill and New South Head roads.

The starting point at the top of the road is between two girls' schools: on the Rose Bay side, **Kambala Church of England Girls' School** ❷ and, on the opposing side, the splendid Catholic **Kincoppal Rose Bay, School of the Sacred Heart** ❸. Kambala is based around a house originally known as 'Tivoli'. The initial builder was the well-connected Captain William Dumaresque, Governor Darling's brother-in-law and Alexander Macleay's (see Walk 1, page 11) son-in-law. His stone cottage was redesigned into an elegant house in the 1880s by architect J. Horbury Hunt for its new owner, Maurice Black. In 1912, Miss Gurney and Mademoiselle Soubbeiran moved their school here from Bellevue Hill, bringing the name 'Kambala' with it. The school went up for sale in 1923 but, assisted by prominent locals, re-emerged as a Church of England girls' school.

The Sacred Heart school across the street was also a Horbury Hunt design. In 1880 Hunt had redesigned the house 'Claremont', built for George Thorne in 1852. Two years later, the Sisters of the Sacred Heart, a French order, leased the house and remaining grounds as a convent. Hunt was again commissioned, this time to build the main five-storey convent structure between 1884 and 1888. Then, in 1897, he designed the great chapel, considered his finest work. The order's school, 'Kincoppal', moved here in 1970 (see Walk 1).

Canadian-born John Horbury Hunt (1838–1904), was working in Boston when the American Civil War broke out. Architectural commissions dried up so Hunt left for India, but during a Sydney stopover, Colonial Architect James Barnet persuaded him to stay. He worked for Edmund Blacket before branching out on his own in 1869. His work was fresh and original, making strong use of natural materials. An eccentric and argumentative man, Hunt saw his business collapse in the 1890s depression; he died a poverty-stricken recluse in 1904 (see Walk 6).

At the bottom of Bayview Hill Road, a turn to the right leads to the signposted Hermitage Foreshore Track, starting between the last houses. From 1905, a community pressure group, the Harbour Foreshores Vigilance Committee, lobbied governments about the loss of harbour-side land to private ownership. Consequently, the government purchased this strip of foreshore in 1912, a year after Nielsen Park had also been purchased for public use. The first kilometre or so of the track dips up and down along the narrow reserve, past a succession of little bays, beaches and headlands with constantly wonderful views across Rose Bay and occasional seaplanes buzzing past (see feature box, page 42). Rose Bay itself, Sydney Harbour's largest bay, was named by Governor Arthur Phillip to honour

Sir George Rose, British Secretary to the Treasury.

The quiet **cemetery** 4 of the Sisters of the Sacred Heart Convent is soon passed—note the Hunt-designed stone Celtic cross of Reverend Mother Febronie Vercruyss (d.1895), founder of the convent. Soon the walk drops to a boardwalk lined with coral trees behind Queens Beach. Public and private tracks occasionally enter the narrow reserve strip—initially dominated by introduced plants—from the right.

At Hermit Point, the reserve widens around the headland onto Hermit Bay with pathways, picnic tables, boat ramp and wharf—a pleasant spot to pause before continuing along the track. Once beyond and above the Hermit Bay beach, look back to the houses now on the opposite side, and especially the many rustic Gothic gables of **'The Hermitage'** 5. This house gave the walk and the little bay it overlooks their names. It began as a smaller cottage, built by Alexander Dick around 1837 and later occupied by Edward Mason Hunt (who may have been the 'hermit'). It grew steadily and was remodelled and enlarged by architect Emil Sodersten after it had been badly damaged by fire in 1936. Used as a bank training college in the 1960s, it is again privately owned.

Soon after Hermit Bay, the narrow strip of foreshore walk reaches a large, cleared area with a great white house at the head of the lawns, its grand, bowed entrance facing the harbour. **'Carrara'** 6 (named after the Italian marble used in it, and later called 'Strickland House') was built on a portion of the Wentworth estate given to Wentworth's daughter, Thomasine, as part of a marriage settlement but sold to Charles Lowe in 1854. The house, designed by John Frederick Hilly, was sold before its completion in 1856 to John Hosking, Sydney's first elected mayor. Its original two-storey coach house and servants' quarters stand nearby. After Hosking's death, 'Carrara' went through several prominent owners. It was a school and then, after its purchase by the government in 1914, became Strickland Women's Convalescent Home, opened in 1915 to relieve pressure on general hospitals during World War I. Additional buildings were added to the hospital and the grounds were landscaped in the 1930s—notice the bowling greens in the gully. Closure of the hospital in 1989 opened the building to controversy about its future use and government proposals to lease it as a 'boutique' hotel remain the subject of local protest.

Walk back down to the foreshore, where the track continues above two more small and natural beaches, Tingara and Milk, the latter with a tessellated rock pavement. As Nielsen Park is entered, coastal bushland replaces introduced species. A track leads up to the right, to the main roadway, but the more interesting way is to continue ahead, past rocky outcrops, water views and through the bush before making a short climb to the road. Nielsen Park was named in 1912 for Niels Rasmus Wilson Nielsen (1869–1930), Copenhagen-born Labor Minister for Lands, 1910–1911. A dedicated and sincere socialist, Nielsen reacquired harbourside land for public use under his Foreshores Resumption Scheme —Taronga Park and Nielsen Park being his most important successes. Nielsen Park

Rose Bay, Nielsen Park, Vaucluse ☼ 11

Walk 5 Key

- **S** Start
- **1** View point
- **2** 'Kambala'
- **3** Kincoppal/Sacred Heart school
- **4** Convent cemetery
- **5** 'The Hermitage'
- **6** 'Carrara'
- **7** Steel Point fortifications
- **8** 'Greycliffe'
- **9** Point Seymour Light
- **10** 'Greenway'
- **11** Garden 'lighthouse'
- **12** St Michael's church

Boats that Flew

In July 1938 the true era of Australian international air travel dawned with a tri-weekly Sydney to London air service from the new Rose Bay Water Airport. The aircraft, jointly operated by Qantas and British Empire Airways, were Short S23 C Class Empire Flying Boats. Qantas had six, its first called 'Cooee'. About half of Rose Bay's Lyne Park became the ground base with tarmac, hangars, workshops, terminal and control tower.

The great birds lumbered elegantly across Rose Bay, lifting steadily to begin their 10-day flight to the UK. Travelling at around 250 kilometres per hour, their 15 passengers enjoyed cabins and sleeping accommodation, lounges and promenades, and pursers serving excellent meals. Along the way the planes landed 29 times to refuel with the odd overnight stop at hotels such as Singapore's Raffles.

During World War II the base's role was predominantly military, operating US and RAAF flying boats. On 16 September 1945, the first Australian POWs to return from Japanese captivity landed here amidst emotional scenes. After the war, larger seaplanes cut the journey to less than six days. In the 1950s, long-range land-based passenger aircraft brought the elegant flying boat era to an end. The last commercial seaplane service, to Lord Howe Island, was discontinued when an airfield opened on the island in 1974. Today, Rose Bay is used by small float planes carrying sightseers and a few commuters.

Rose Bay seaplanes, with the Sacred Heart Convent above.

was incorporated into Sydney Harbour National Park when the latter was created in 1975, and the Hermitage Foreshore was added in 1984.

Almost immediately ahead is a Commonwealth degaussing station for naval vessels (degaussing is a countermeasure against magnetic mines) and beyond it the **Steel Point fortifications** 7. These 1871 emplacements originally held three 80-pounder muzzle-loaders, replaced in the 1890s with 5-inch breech-loading guns. The site fell into disuse after 1910.

Follow the signs towards the National Parks District Office, the romantically steep-pitched rustic Gothic and gabled **'Greycliffe'** 8. Completed in 1862, it is set in idyllic bushland overlooking Shark Beach. Its design, like neighbouring 'Carrara', is attributed to John Frederick Hilly, and it too was a William Charles Wentworth wedding gift, this time for daughter Fanny and her husband John Reeve, a Gippsland grazier. They probably never lived there and 'Greycliffe' was leased as a home by Joseph Scaife Willis (1808–97), a merchant and businessman. It was also owned for a few years by Sir John Robertson (1816–91), Premier of New South Wales (see feature box, page 57). The Foreshores Resumption Scheme acquired it in 1911 and the grounds of the house were opened to public use. The house became, in 1913, the Lady Edeline Hospital for Babies (named, like its neighbour two years later, after Governor Strickland's wife). Its main purpose was to care for infants suffering from gastroenteritis. From 1934 until 1968, 'Greycliffe' was a Tresillian Mothercraft Home, providing support for new mothers. It is now the Sydney District National Parks Office and visitors are welcome to visit the ground floor display, Monday to Friday.

From 'Greycliffe', it is easy to walk down to ominously named Shark Beach. There is a large netted swimming enclosure, in summer only, and an early twentieth-century bathing shed and kiosk behind the beach. In summer, the beach and grounds gather crowds of bathers and picnickers. Beyond the men's changing shed, steps uphill past the women's shed join a grassy path towards Vaucluse Point. On the way, look back from the clifftops for views of the city and of 'Greycliffe' amongst the trees above the beach. Across the harbour is more of Sydney Harbour National Park, with Clifton Gardens and Georges and Middle heads.

Little grassy groves between trees lead out to the point above the curious rocky islet called Bottle & Glass Rocks, a name given in 1799, before target practice from passing warships shattered the rocks' shape. Watsons Bay is straight ahead, but nearer, to the right, is Vaucluse Bay. Look across its mouth to see a delicate, minaret-like **'lighthouse'** 9 at Point Seymour. Note, too, the plethora of channel markers out in the harbour. Harbour navigation can be trickier than it looks and the concealed Sow and Pigs Reef nearby trapped several ships before more sophisticated navigation aids were developed.

Follow the groves and track around towards Coolong Road, past opulent waterfront houses, to the park gates. Notice the stone lodge in the park as you begin along Greycliffe Avenue—a small evocation of 'Greycliffe'.

At the junction with Vaucluse Road, turn left and then right into Wentworth Avenue. Many houses are attention-grabbers, such as the Spanish Mission-style hacienda at number 54. The style, with its Hollywood associations, was popular in the middle-class eastern suburbs between the wars.

Uphill, at number 24 on the corner of Fisher Avenue, is an example of the more restrained Mediterranean style introduced to Australia by architect Leslie Wilkinson. This 1923 house, **'Greenway'** ⑩, the first Australian example of the style, was Wilkinson's own home. He had come to Australia in 1918 as the first Professor of Architecture at Sydney University and immediately recognised the style's appropriateness to Sydney's climate.

A little further up Wentworth, past the Gilliver Avenue junction, look for number 12, where another minaret-like **'lighthouse'** ⑪ stands in the garden. This 1880s red navigation light, in conjunction with the Point Seymour light visible from Vaucluse Point, marks the harbour's eastern channel. Return to Gilliver Avenue. Here, number 11A was built in 1936 by architects Crick and Wells as a demonstration of the modern Functionalist style (new to Australia) and was bought by Kings Theatre entrepreneur, Herbert Roberts. Near Vaucluse Road, visit **St Michael's church** ⑫, with its warm, rusticated stonework, shingle roof and stunning harbour views. Begun in 1877 by architect Edmund Blacket, added to between 1907 and 1910 by his son Cyril, it was completed—with spire—between 1928 and 1938 by Leslie Wilkinson. The spire was replaced in 1969.

Now turn left into Vaucluse Road with the elegant architecture of Barat-Burn, Kincoppal's primary school, on one side, and the expensive real estate of the Kincoppal tennis courts on the other. The original house 'Claremont' can be seen, now part of the main school/convent building. New South Head and Bayview Hill roads and the end of the walk are ahead, together with 'that view', so well worth enjoying one more time.

Walk 6

Commanding Heights
Vaucluse

In Provence, the River Sorgue bursts dramatically from beneath the ground at the ancient village of Fontaine-de-Vaucluse, which nestles gently against a rocky plateau known as the Vaucluse. And just what that has to do with a prosperous Sydney harbourside suburb is not immediately obvious. But it, too, will emerge.

Additional Reading
John Ritchie *The Wentworths: Father and Son*, Melbourne University Press, 1997.

Background: Sydney's guiding light for almost two centuries—the Macquarie Light.

Features
Clifftop and harbourside scenery • historic sites and parks, including Vaucluse House.

Distance
Approx. 5km • links with walks 5 and 7.

Time
2 hours.

Difficulty
Easy to moderate • some steps • Vaucluse Park OK for strollers and wheelchairs.

Access
Old and New South Head roads buses (Watsons Bay) • street parking. UBD: Map 238 C1 Gregory's: Map 348 H1.

Facilities
Toilets at South Head Cemetery, Vaucluse House, Parsley Bay • picnic spots at Vaucluse Reserve, Parsley Bay. Shops at New South Head Road.

46 ✸ Sydney Strolls ⚓ Eastern Suburbs

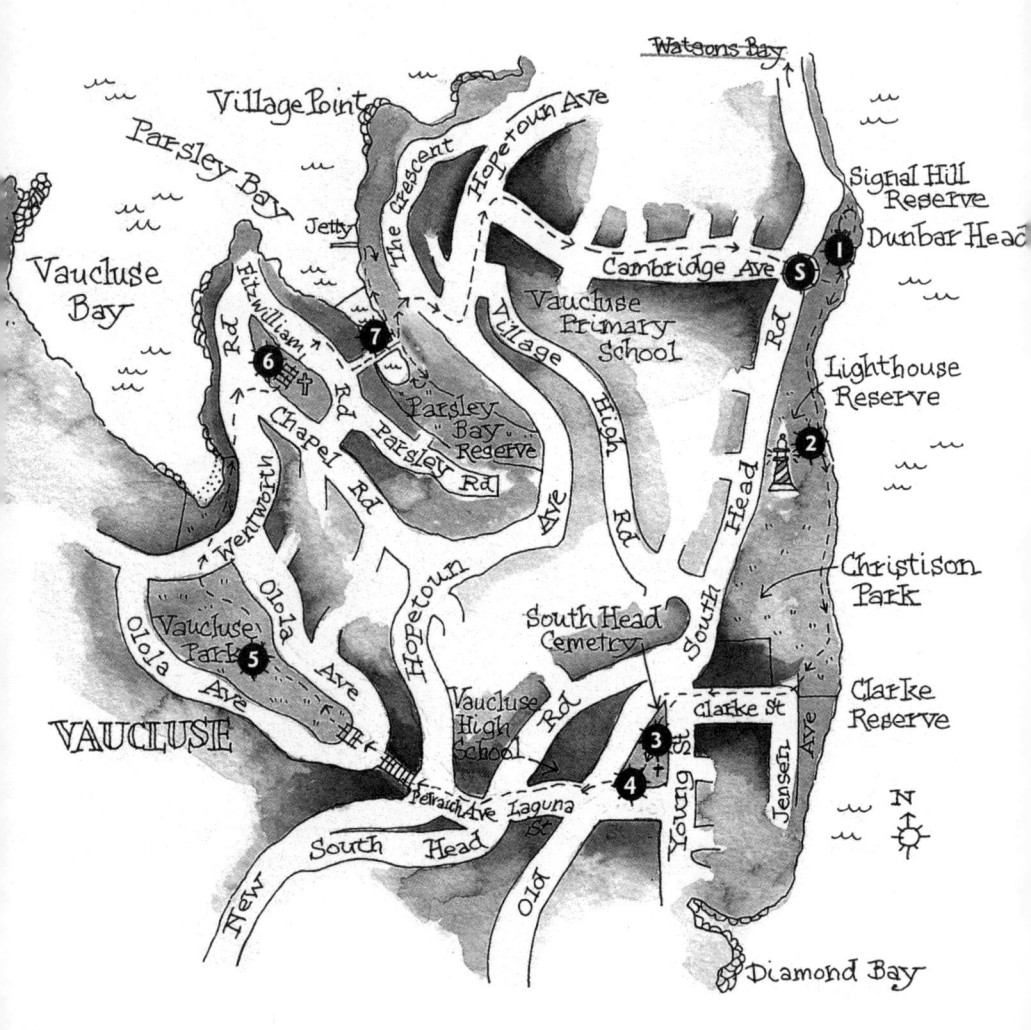

Walk 6 Key

- **S** Start
- **1** Signal Station
- **2** Macquarie Light
- **3** Sir Walter Davidson's grave
- **4** Fairfax graves
- **5** Vaucluse House
- **6** Wentworth's mausoleum
- **7** Parsley Bay suspension bridge

Either or both walks 5 and 7 could be linked to this walk for a varied and invigorating day. This walk begins in Old South Head Road opposite Cambridge Avenue, above the ocean and outside the **Signal Station** ❶—not to be confused with the Macquarie Light. On the corner of Cambridge Avenue is a house which, in 1853, was the Family Hotel—the families of the time mostly being those of pilots, fishermen or lighthouse keepers.

Take a ramble around the old Signal Station, now used by the volunteer Coast Guard. The coastal views are spectacular and the view down harbour reveals the reason for the station's location—a direct line of sight back to Sydney Cove. The central tower of the station was designed in 1842 by the Colonial Architect, Mortimer Lewis. In maritime Sydney, the station had enormous importance. Governor Phillip had a flagpole erected here in January 1790 to signal when approaching ships were sighted. Two years into the new Sydney settlement, with the colonists near starvation, their hopes rested on the arrival of supplies from England. On 3 June a signal was raised but the excitement collapsed when the ship proved to be the *Lady Juliana*, carrying starving women convicts and bringing the news that the accompanying supply ship, *Guardian*, had been wrecked. Three more convict ships arrived the same month—more than a quarter of the 1000 convicts aboard having died en route while the ships' masters hoarded food to sell at inflated prices in Sydney. Economic rationalism had made its entrance into Australia. The Signal Station's importance was underlined by the line of semaphore signalling stations which stretched from here to Parramatta by the 1820s, and again in 1858, when New South Wales's first electric telegraph line was installed to link the station with central Sydney.

Signal Hill Fort was established next to it in 1893. The main gun was a hydro pneumatic 9.2-inch breech-loader which popped up above its emplacement to fire, then recoiled downwards, back out of sight. There were similar guns further south (see Walks 9 and 13). Last fired in 1933, it was removed in 1937 and its 22-tonne barrel now rests in Victoria Barracks (see feature box, page 29). Two 6-inch Mk II coastal defence guns replaced it as part of Sydney's World War II anti-ship defences (see Walk 12, page 84), but they, too, became obsolete in the face of modern weaponry and were removed in the 1960s. The underground fort is now locked up.

Now return south and continue past the Signal Station along the path towards the **Macquarie Light** ❷. Governor Macquarie had a lighthouse—the first in Australia—built here between 1816 and 1818, and was so pleased with convict architect Francis Greenway's elegant design, that he gave Greenway a pardon. By the 1880s the building's sandstone was crumbling and the lantern was to be replaced with an electric light (the first in an Australian lighthouse). A new and taller lighthouse, similar in design to Greenway's, was built behind the first which was then demolished. The new one came into service in 1883 and could be seen 40 kilometres out to sea. Beyond the lighthouse, the path south through Christison Park reveals cliffs dipping towards Diamond Bay with the old sewer vent for the Bondi Ocean Outfall Sewer gracing a distant headland. At Clarke Street, off Clarke Reserve, turn right and enter South Head Cemetery near the junction of Old and New South Head roads.

This compact, well-tended cemetery contains some interesting souls. Near the services building, note the dominant **Celtic cross** ❸ raised by public subscription for Sir Walter Davidson (1859–1923), who died in office while Governor of New South Wales. Sir Walter, whose life began and was largely spent in far-flung posts of the then great British Empire, presided with impeccable constitutional impartiality over one of the most remarkable days in New South Wales politics. On 20 December 1921, Labor Premier James Dooley's government was defeated in the Legislative Assembly and he resigned. Davidson refused to dissolve Parliament and appointed opposition leader Sir George Fuller as Premier. Seven hours later Fuller was defeated. He also sought a dissolution, but as Dooley clearly now again had a majority in the House, Davidson refused. Fuller resigned and Dooley was sworn in again. Three governments in a little over seven hours.

Two rows towards Old South Head Road lies another former Government House occupant, Lady Helen Cutler (1923–90), wife of the State's longest-serving Governor (from 1966 to 1981), Sir Roden Cutler VC (b.1916). The avenue where Sir Walter rests has since been filled with smaller memorials, but further south along it stands the Packer family tomb. This includes Robert Clyde Packer (1879–1934), the family's original tough and controversial newspaperman. Editor or owner of several papers, including the feisty *Smith's Weekly*, he became managing editor of Associated Newspapers. His son, the legendary Sir Frank (1906–74), who lies here together with his wife, Gretel, launched the *Australian Women's Weekly* in 1933. Its phenomenal success enabled the creation of Australian Consolidated Press in 1936, the empire entering television in 1955 with Channel 9. Sir Frank shared his father's enthusiasm for yachting, and undertook Australia's first challenges for the America's Cup with Gretel I and Gretel II in 1962 and 1970. Sir Frank's empire, in turn, laid the foundation for son Kerry's further business expansions.

Just beyond is a distinctive rusticated stone stump, the last resting place of Sir John Robertson (1816–91), three times Premier of New South Wales (see feature box, page 57). The tomb was designed by J. Horbury Hunt (1838–1904), an imaginative Canadian-born architect who left his mark on the eastern suburbs (see Walk 5, page 38). Hunt left little to mark the nearby low brick mound in which he is buried. A small mosaic panel at one side is marked 'JHH, 1895', the date referring not to Hunt's own death but to that of his wife, Elizabeth, who lies here also.

Down near the arched stone gateway on Old South Head Road are more media barons. A simple Celtic cross on a grassed enclosure memorialises the **Fairfaxes** ❹, of the *Sydney Morning Herald*. John Fairfax, who originally built up the *Herald*, is not here, but the next three generations (all knighted) are: son Sir James Reading Fairfax (1834–1919); his son Sir James Oswald (1863–1928); and, in turn, his

Wentworth of Vaucluse

William Charles Wentworth (1790–1872) might well be the single-most important figure in New South Wales colonial history. His father, D'Arcy, a medical practitioner, was strongly encouraged to emigrate after facing charges of highway robbery. Aboard ship he took up with convict Catherine Crowley, and W. C. was born as the ship approached Norfolk Island.

D'Arcy prospered and young William was sent to school in England. During one return to Sydney in 1813, he joined the first party of Europeans to cross the Blue Mountains. Back in England he studied law and published a book promoting New South Wales. On his return to the colony in the 1820s he soon became the leading advocate for representative self-government, freedom of the press, trial by jury, state-provided education and native-born Australians. He co-founded and edited Australia's first independent newspaper, the *Australian*, in 1824, battling acrimoniously with Governor Darling over freedom of the press and other issues. As Darling departed the colony in 1831, Wentworth held a celebratory party for 4000 at 'Vaucluse'.

Wentworth played a major part in gaining New South Wales's first elected legislature in 1843 and led the drawing-up of the constitution which brought responsible government in 1856. A leading 'emancipist'—supporting the rights of former convicts—he married Sarah Cox, daughter of a former convict, in 1829. Sarah suffered social ostracism amongst colonial 'society', which contributed to the couple's move to England in 1857. Never a radical democrat, Wentworth's conservatism increased with age and property. A complex and often contradictory man, he, nonetheless, led the way to contemporary Australian democracy.

Resting on the rock of another age
—W. C. Wentworth's mausoleum.

son, Sir Warwick Oswald (1901–87). All were directors and proprietors of John Fairfax Ltd, and their diverse interests over the generations included business, the military, yachting, motoring, charities, farming, music, art, travel, philosophy, and play writing. Golf was another enduring interest and Sir James Oswald died the classic golfer's death on the Royal Sydney links at Rose Bay.

Cross Old South Head Road to Vaucluse High School, turn right down Laguna Street, and cross New South Head Road to lane-like Petrarch Avenue. Harbour views open up as Patrarch drops to Hopetoun Avenue, named for Australia's first Governor-General, Lord Hopetoun. The descent continues to Olola Avenue where steps plunge through ferns to meet a stream emerging from the ground into the Vaucluse House Reserve. This area and the street name 'Petrarch' provide, at last, the clue to the suburb's naming. The 14th-century Italian poet, Petrarch, spent many years at Fontaine-de-Vaucluse—where the River Sorgue surges from beneath the ground—writing wrenchingly of his absent love, Laura.

In 1803 this emerging stream may have evoked the image of Petrarch's isolation and lost love in the mind of Sir Henry Brown Hayes. Hayes purchased 105 acres (42.5 hectares) here for a farm, which he named 'Vaucluse', and built an eight-room cottage. Sir Henry was, despite title and property, a convict, transported from Ireland in 1801 for the crime of abducting an heiress whom he was convinced was in love with him. She, apparently, was less convinced. Nonetheless, this absent love seemed to cause Hayes to identify with Petrarch. Being a wealthy convict, however, had its compensations, and Sir Henry lived comfortably at 'Vaucluse', indulging his curiously romantic traits. Plagued by snakes as well as absent loves and aware that St Patrick had banished snakes from Irish soil, he imported 153 tonnes of Irish turf and had it laid about the house as a snake barrier. After receiving a pardon in 1812, Sir Henry left the colony and Vaucluse became part of Captain Piper's huge estate (see feature box, page 36).

After Piper's demise, William Charles Wentworth (see feature box, page 49), bought 'Vaucluse' in 1827 and greatly enlarged it, adding the characteristic castellated Gothic appearance to the house. He enlarged the estate five-fold until it spread across 240 hectares of waterfront land, but began subdividing again as early as 1838.

Most was subdivided by 1910 when the New South Wales Government decided to buy **'Vaucluse House'** ★ and the remaining area around it, opening the house as a memorial to the 'father of the Constitution' in 1924. A visit to the house's elegant interior is almost essential, but the 10-hectare reserve is just as important, with its mixture of formal gardens, paddock, lawns and outbuildings such as the washhouse and the 1829 Gothic stables.

From the front gates of the park, cross Wentworth Road to the waterfront where the stream empties into rock-fringed Vaucluse Bay. This natural, relaxing little public reserve was also bought by the State in 1910. From its north-eastern end follow Wentworth Road past some of the area's distinctive homes to Chapel Road.

A short way up Chapel Road a small Gothic chapel on the left seems to rise from a rock. This is **W. C. Wentworth's mausoleum** ❻, at the rock known to the family as 'Papa's rock'. He often viewed the harbour from hereabouts, and after his death in England he was brought home to this resting place, later shared by other Wentworths. After looking into the simple interior of the chapel, built by the Mansfield Brothers between 1873 and 1874, climb the steps behind to the contrasting Wentworth Memorial church designed by Donald Gazzard and eventually built in 1965 on land Wentworth had left for the purpose. Continue down the front steps and driveway into Fitzwilliam Road, turn right and, after about 100 metres, take the lane that leads off to the left to Parsley Bay Reserve.

The lane suddenly emerges onto the wonderful wooden **suspension bridge** ❼ over Parsley Bay, completed in 1910 to the design of the Vaucluse Town Clerk, Edwin Sautelle. This delightful reserve and its bushland trails are worth exploring. An easterly path leads from the other side of the bridge alongside the long, shallow inlet to the beach, the kiosk and other facilities, while a path in the opposite direction takes you to a jetty at the bay's mouth.

Back at the bridgehead, the path leads up through more reserve to The Crescent, where a short walk to the right takes you to Hopetoun Avenue again. About 400 metres north along Hopetoun Avenue towards Watsons Bay, turn right into Cambridge Avenue. This tree-lined street begins with an attractive stone home combining several styles, and pleasant Victorian and Federation homes, then grows narrower and steeper after a dogleg at Vaucluse Primary School as it rises to Old South Head Road and the walk's end.

Walk 7

Walls of Stone
Watsons Bay

Features:
Spectacular clifftop and harbour scenery • historic and military sites • nautical history • historic buildings.

Distance
Approx. 4½ km • links to Walk 6.

Time
1½–2 hours.

Difficulty
Easy to moderate • steps and many inclines • limited stroller and wheelchair access.

Access
Watsons Bay buses and ferries; street parking (difficult on weekends). UBD: Map 218 A14 Gregory's: Map 318 F14.

Facilities
Toilets at Fishermans Wharf, Camp Cove, Robertson Park, Gap Bluff Centre; picnic spots at Laings Point, Robertson Park • shops and restaurants. No dogs in national park.

Robert Watson (1756–1819), quartermaster of HMS *Sirius*, became one of Sydney's earliest chief pilots, harbourmaster and the first superintendent of the 1816 Macquarie Light. His name is appropriately recalled in this picturesque former maritime village, which owed its early existence to navigation and fishing, and its dramatic surrounds.

Additional Reading
Cedric Emanuel *Watsons Bay Sketchbook*, Rigby, 1973.
P. R. Stephensen *The History and Description of Sydney Harbour*, Rigby, 1966.

Background: The Gap, crumbling wall between harbour and ocean.

A memorial to **Robert Watson** ❶ stands at the edge of the park near Fishermans Wharf. The first of the eastern suburbs to be settled, Watsons Bay remained a tiny marine village of fisherfolk, lighthouse keepers and harbour pilots until late into the 19th century. It was not until the interwar years that the rest of the eastern suburbs finally crept up to it. However, the area was always a popular excursion destination, even more so when ferries, and then trams, improved access. Watsons Bay offers a walk packed with natural spectacle and history; the elements, whether sunny or wild, contributing to the drama. But take care not to become part of the drama—these cliffs have taken many lives.

The walk begins at **Fisherman's Wharf** ❷ amidst a concentration of seafood eateries, but with resolve (and lack of funds) you can safely pass along the beachfront promenade to the steps at the end which lead up into Cove Street. Cove Street's eastern side is probably the most charming part of this little group of tiny streets making up a small-scale marine village where a sense of an earlier time survives. Number 17, with its dormer windows, is probably the oldest of what were once pilots', sailors' and fishermen's cottages. Turn left into Pacific Street, past more diminutive homes, although here the ever-present threat of development is apparent. When the cul-de-sac at the end is reached, look for the memorial plaques on the last house on the Camp Cove side. It was originally a **marine biology station** ❸ established in 1880 by the eminent Russian scientist, Nicholas de Mikluoho-Maclay (see feature box, page 57). From either side of the cul-de-sac at the top of Laings (or Green) Point make your way down to the harbour vista.

Edward Laing was given the first land grant in the area in 1793. A **memorial** ❹ commemorates the first harbour landing here by Europeans on 21 January 1788, led by Captain Arthur Phillip, but the documentary evidence for Camp Cove being the actual place is ambiguous. Laings Point is also significant for its military history. A bunker and remnants of old defences can be seen—the South Head area is honeycombed with gun emplacements and observation posts from various eras between the 1870s and 1960s. The coastline between here and the Signal Station (see Walk 6, page 45) housed up to 25 pieces of coastal artillery, as well as an artillery school until after World War II. During World War II, Laings Point was also the eastern end of Sydney Harbour's anti-submarine boom—essentially 1480 metres of mesh strung on a line of piles between Laings Point and Georges Head, with openable 'gates' to allow ships through. A **plaque** ❺ on the point provides excellent information. Begun in early 1942, it was only partially completed by 31 May 1942 when three Japanese midget submarines slipped into the harbour, launched from a fleet of five large submarines offshore. Two managed to get through the incomplete boom but one got tangled in it and the submarine's two-man crew blew themselves up. The other two subs caused widespread alarm for a time before being destroyed, one torpedoing the *Kuttabul* (see walks 1 and 4).

Steps lead down to Camp Cove beach with its older-world ambience, and from

54 ✵ Sydney Strolls & Eastern Suburbs

Walk 7 Key

- **S** Start
- **1** Robert Watson memorial
- **2** Fishermans Wharf
- **3** Former marine biology station
- **4** Arthur Phillip memorial
- **5** Anti-submarine boom plaque
- **6** Gun in emplacement
- **7** Hornby Light
- **8** Former Officers' Mess
- **9** Practice battery remnants
- **10** Dunbar anchor
- **11** St Peters church
- **12** Former Watsons Bay schoolhouse
- **13** Watsons Bay Pilot Station
- **14** Roadmakers' memorial
- **15** Site of 'Clovelly'

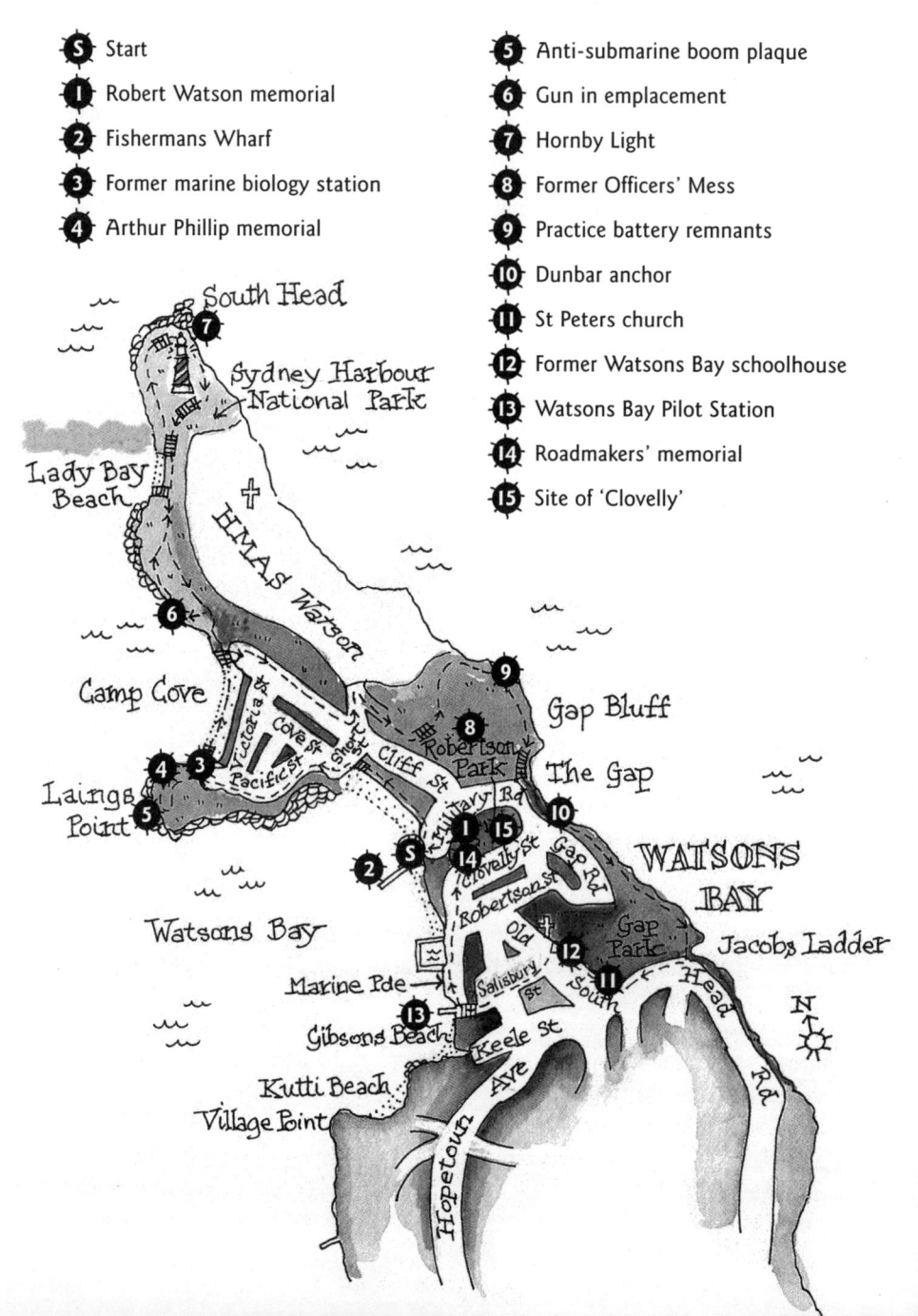

its northern end more steps lead up to part of Sydney Harbour National Park. Notice the elegant, verandahed cottage above the north end of the beach, originally the quarters of the artillery school's Chief Instructor. Beyond the steps, take the stone-paved ramp (once linked to a military wharf) past walls and rock faces with rifle slits, to a **gun emplacement** **6**. Part of the 1873 Inner Battery, this still mounts a 12-tonne, 9-inch RML (rifled muzzle loader) gun, one of five at this battery until 1895. From the front of the gun, a safe clifftop path passes along firing walls and up to a bitumen road before entering the bush alongside HMAS Watson's fence. Steps drop to Lady Bay Beach, one of Sydney Harbour's two nude beaches. An earlier name for the beach was Ladies' Haul Beach. It was popular last century with ladies from the military base, but its steep approaches meant they had to be hauled up or down by rope.

Beyond Lady Bay Beach, the path rises to the rocky platform of South Head, meeting first the two 1858 keepers houses and then the **Hornby Light** **7**. Near the first house is an unfinished gun emplacement begun in 1853. Other emplacements bristle across the area before the back gates of HMAS Watson are reached. Most were built in the 1870s but some were remodelled in World War II when two 6-inch Mark 7 breach-loading guns were installed. A searchlight emplacement survives just south of the lighthouse.

The cliffs are unfenced and have claimed many lives—most more or less intentionally—so treat them with caution, especially in windy conditions. The cliffs nearby were also responsible for Sydney's worst shipwreck, that of the 1347-tonne clipper *Dunbar*, in 1857. The wreck occurred on a storm-wracked August night, when the ship's master mistook The Gap for the harbour entrance. The spot was so isolated that Sydney was unaware of the disaster until well into the next day. One crewman, from the 122 passengers and crew, survived, struggling up the cliff face to safety 30 hours later. Two months afterwards, the 904-tonne clipper *Catherine Adamson* was wrecked on North Head with 21 lives lost. The striped Hornby Light was built in response to these disasters and one of the first lighthouse keepers was James Johnston, solitary survivor of the *Dunbar*.

Near the HMAS Watson back gates, steps lead down to the return path past Lady Bay Beach. Follow the track back to Camp Cove and the northern end of the beach and then along Cliff Street about 200 metres before taking a sharp left towards HMAS Watson's main entrance. This base was commissioned in 1945 as a radar training school and is now an advanced anti-submarine, navigation and warfare training centre. There are some interesting pieces of hardware near the gate. Its clifftop chapel, dedicated in 1962, can often be visited, so check at the gate if you are interested.

Slightly before the base's guardhouse, follow the branch road (signposted 'Sydney Harbour National Park, Gap Bluff Centre') off to the right. This road emerges from the bush into a large open space fringed with several interesting buildings. An army base from 1894 to 1981, this was for decades the army's School of Artillery, subsequently shifted to North

Head. A small toilet block survives from the wooden barracks blocks that once lined this parade ground. Ahead, the few other remaining buildings from the original 30 or so include a low brick building called 'The Armoury' and an 1890s weatherboard cottage. The most interesting building is the large 1930s P&O style **former Officers' Mess** 8, an unusual look for military architecture. This area is entirely accessible to the public, but the buildings are leased to a private management school.

Enter the bush immediately left of 'The Armoury' up steps which climb towards HMAS Watson's fence again. Just beyond an old storehouse, turn away from the fence, following the cliffside path southwards. Here you might notice the low clifftop emplacements of an 1894 **practice battery** 9. During World War II, there was a radar station and many buildings here, but the remnants of military landscaping are now rapidly disappearing into the bush. The natural views from the Bluff area are wonderful and get better when the whole dip of The Gap and the cliffs sweeping southwards open up spectacularly below.

Seen from here, The Gap, with a crush of fallen rock at its base, appears as a crumbling weak spot in the defensive wall of cliffs protecting the city and harbour. There are sea caves under the cliff and erosion will eventually bring the sea through into the harbour—though that might be some time away yet. The sandstone in these cliffs was laid as sediment more than 200 million years ago in the Triassic period. In the Jurassic period, 40 million years later, some cataclysmic event resulted in an enormous crack forming, which erosion and time have turned into Sydney's cliff line.

From these heights, for several days following 20 August 1857, helpless spectators watched as the waves threw bodies and wreckage from the *Dunbar* onto the rock platform below. The **Dunbar anchor** 10 has been placed at the southern end of The Gap as a memorial. The Gap's association with death and despair, unfortunately, continues with regular suicide attempts (successful and not), accidents, fishermen in trouble, and the occasional murder. It was The Gap's notorious record that led to the formation in the 1930s of the first Police Cliff Rescue unit.

The path continues upward through Gap Park, past more gun platforms. The harbour and seaward views are stunning, but it is also worth noting little **St Peter's church** 11 perched inland above the low coastal vegetation. There is also a well-concealed parallel path, starting behind The Gap near the bus turning circle, which has no real view but passes pleasantly and very evenly through the bushes. This is part of the slightly dangerous 1909–60 Watsons Bay tramline. Immediately before climbing to Old South Head Road, note the clefts in the rock dropping seaward. Known as Jacob's Ladder, after the rope ladders used here by fishermen, these are actually chines, or eroded volcanic dykes.

At Old South Head Road, leave nature's stonework and head downhill towards the warm human-hewn stone and the wooden shingles of St Peter's church, designed by Edmund Blacket in 1864. Named after the 'pilot of Galilee' it has long been associated with the harbour pilots. The church gates memorialise the *Greycliffe* ferry disaster of 1927, in which 40 passengers—many of them schoolchildren—died after the ferry was run down by the steamship *Tahiti*. The church's organ loft was added in 1902 and houses an organ with an extraordinary history. Made in London in 1796 for the Chancellor of the Exchequer, Spencer Perceval, the organ was loaned to Napoleon Bonaparte during his stay on Elba after Perceval had been assassinated in 1812. Napoleon escaped back to France

Sir John & the Head Scientist

Sir John Robertson (1816–91), born in Scotland, arrived in Sydney with his watchmaker father and family in 1820. A cleft palate and the resulting speech impediment failed to prevent Robertson from being five times Premier of New South Wales. A determined democrat, he supported male suffrage, secret ballot, equal electorates, national education and free trade. As Secretary for Lands he opened western lands to small-scale free selection, breaking the monopoly of the squatter–pastoralists. The Robertsons lived in 'Greycliffe' (see Walk 5, page 38) for some years but 'Clovelly' at Watsons Bay was their longer-term abode, where they developed gardens regarded as second only to the Botanic Gardens.

In 1884, Robertson's widowed daughter, Margaret Clark, married eminent Russian scientist Nicholas de Mikluoho-Maclay (1846–88). Mikluoho-Maclay, the first to explore the north coast of New Guinea, had established a marine biology station **3** at Watsons Bay. His wide-ranging scientific pursuits included botany, linguistics, anthropology and the curious Victorian 'science' of phrenology. Mikluoho-Maclay came to Australia at the invitation of William Macleay, the major contributor to Sydney University's Macleay Museum, and son of Alexander Macleay (see Walk 1, page 11). At the Macleay Museum, until a couple of decades ago, heads collected for phrenological study still greeted visitors from glass specimen jars. Mikluoho-Maclay died in Russia in 1888, after which Margaret Mikluoho-Maclay and her children returned to 'Clovelly'.

Historic Camp Cove seen from alongside the site of Mikluoho-Maclay's former marine biology station.

and met his Waterloo, so the organ went to an English church. Early this century it came to Sydney's Conservatorium of Music. A private owner bought it but soon after World War I it was sold to St Peter's.

Further down the road more fine stone is on offer. Number 272, on the south side of the road, with its circular verandah, is another Edmund Blacket design. Number 333, on The Gap side, with its lovely iron lace, was originally the schoolmaster's residence for the 1876 **Watsons Bay schoolhouse**, ⓬ set back next door and now a Scout Centre. Our Lady Star of the Sea church is next, dating from 1910. A couple of doors further down is an earlier chapel constructed by Portuguese fishermen and pilot boat crews between the 1840s and 1868.

Cross Old South Head Road and take Salisbury Street, with its interesting architectural mix, down to Gibsons Beach. The last part, via a path and steps, emerges at the Watsons Bay **Pilots' Station and wharf** ⓭. The present buildings date from 1959, but the pilots have been at Watsons Bay from the early days. For a time pilotage was a competitive process, pilots racing in cutters to meet incoming ships, until this contributed to accidents. From 1877 to 1959 the pilots operated a series of three steamers, each built at Mort's Dock and each named *Captain Cook*. Diesel-powered boats replaced the last steamer in 1959 and the service was privatised in 1992.

The waterfront walk leads north past the swimming enclosure and a memorial to cliff-rescuer Harry Jenkins, and then to Robertson Park. At Clovelly Street, on the edge of the park, an **obelisk** ⓮ commemorates the construction of the road from Sydney to the Signal Station—supposedly in a remarkable 10 weeks by 21 soldiers of Governor Macquarie's 73rd Regiment. Further into the park is 'Dunbar House' which has had many looks, names and uses since it began life in the 1830s as a house by architect Mortimer Lewis. Now in the restaurant trade, it has been a hotel of several names, the Vaucluse Council Chambers and even a zoo.

Robertson Park, with its palm-lined walk, was the site of **'Clovelly'** ⓯, a house begun in the 1830s by Captain Thomas Watson (unrelated to Robert, see Walk 10, page 71) and subsequently owned or occupied by a string of 19th-century politicians, including two premiers, Sir Henry Parker and Sir John Robertson (see feature box, page 57). The house was demolished in 1903 and the park established three years later.

The wharf, and the end of the walk, lie not far off at the bottom of the park.

Walk 8

Beaches 1

Bondi, Tamarama, Bronte

Bondi Beach has long been a famous icon of life in urban Australia and Sydney—haven for sunlovers and surfers, birthplace of lifesaving, Sydney's holiday at home. On most days, especially the sunny ones, the great kilometre-long curve of sand and rolling breakers, and the cafes and restaurants along Campbell Parade, attract thousands of visitors.

Additional Reading
Robert Drew et al. *Bondi*, James Fraser, 1984.

Background: Mackenzie's Bay, between Bondi and Tamarama beaches forms part of this popular foreshore walk.

Features
Views • famous beaches • leisure and social history • urban growth • architecture • cafes.

Distance
Approx. 4km one way.

Time
1½–2 hours (one way).

Difficulty
Easy, but steps and inclines • strollers could manage throughout, wheelchairs OK at beach sections.

Access
City buses from/to Bondi, Bronte, Bondi Junction • street parking (crowded) or Bondi Beach car park.
UBD: Map 258 B3
Gregory's: Map 378 G3.

Facilities
Shops at Bondi and Bronte beaches • toilets: Bondi, Tamarama, Bronte beaches, Marks Park • picnic areas at Bronte and Tamarama beaches.

60 �֍ Sydney Strolls ✦ Eastern Suburbs

Walk 8 Key

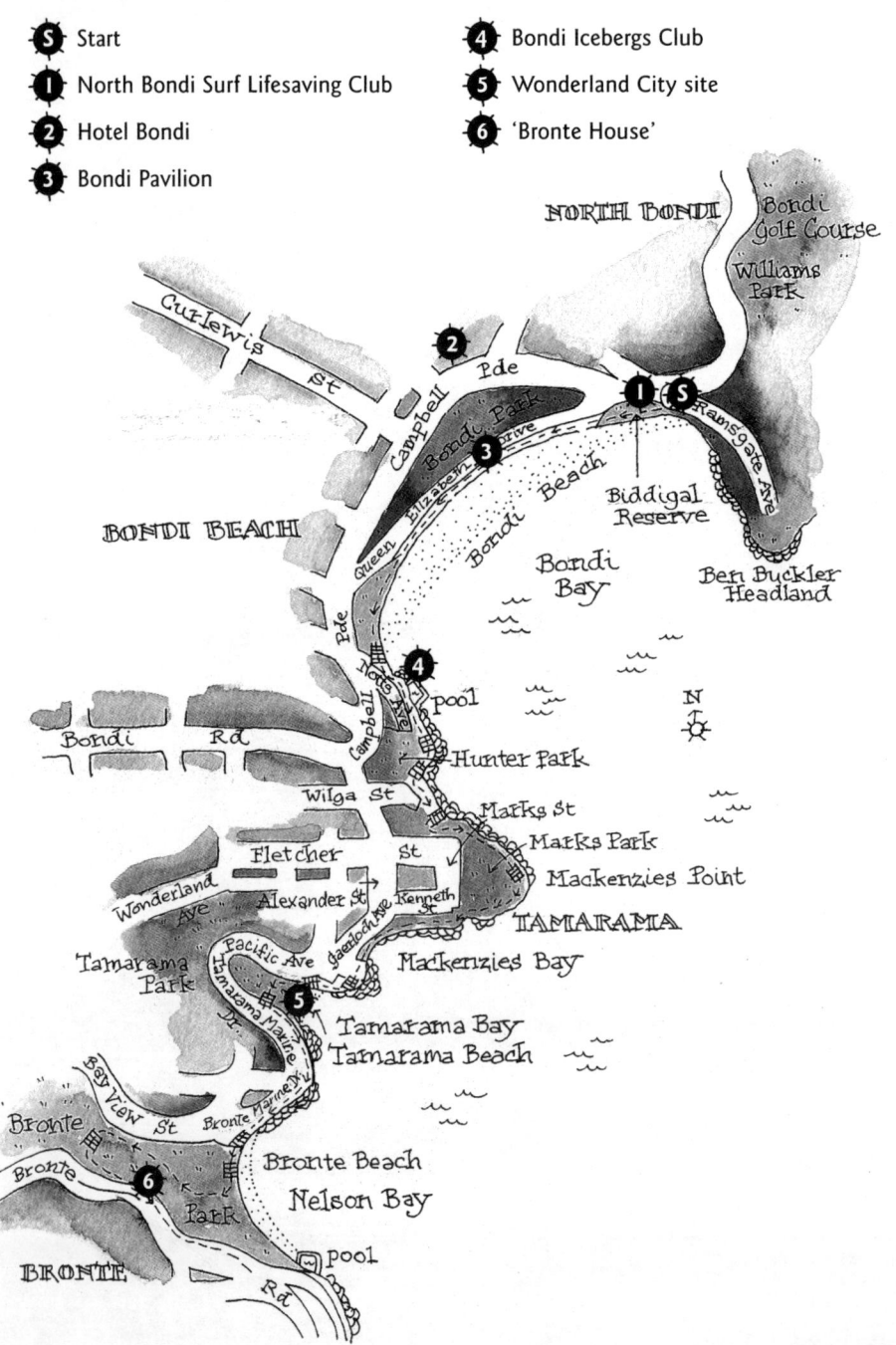

- **S** Start
- **1** North Bondi Surf Lifesaving Club
- **2** Hotel Bondi
- **3** Bondi Pavilion
- **4** Bondi Icebergs Club
- **5** Wonderland City site
- **6** 'Bronte House'

Bondi is Australia's most famous beach, and while the crowds of 100 000 a day of the 1930s are unlikely now, 50 000 local and international visitors on a summer day is common. It is pure Sydney, yet its Mediterranean styles and colours, its low-rise buildings, bars and cafes projecting into the streets, the interwar flats climbing the hillsides and, of course, the arched colonnade of the pavilion, give this quintessentially Australian place a rather Mediterranean feel. In more recent years, its image was somewhat polluted by the sewerage outlet north of the beach, but the extension of the outfall 2 or 3 kilometres out into the ocean in the early 1990s reduced the problem—at least for Bondi.

The walk follows the shoreline along a pathway popular with walkers and joggers. A linear walk, at the end of which buses or a walk back are options, it also links with Walk 9 for those with energy and time. Begin at the northern end of the Beach, at Biddigal Reserve, a name recognising the area's Aboriginal heritage. The Aboriginal name for this place, said to have meant 'noise of water' or 'water breaking over the rocks', was written by Europeans as 'Boondi', 'Bundy' or 'Bundi'. In 1900 storms exposed the area behind the beach, revealing a major archaeological site of Aboriginal artefacts—knives, scrapers, drills, axe heads. But, like the great stretches of sand dunes and the lagoons originally behind the beach, the site disappeared under suburban development. To the north, near the tall 1889 sewer vent, a large set of rock engravings do remain on the edge of the golf course above the cliffs.

The **North Bondi Surf Life Saving Club** ❶ along the beachfront is one of two surf-lifesaving clubs on the beach. Surf-lifesaving and the lifesaving reel were invented at Bondi. Bondi Surf Bathers' Life Saving Club was the first, in 1906, and their first rescue was of a nine-year-old boy, 'Charlie Smith'. Twenty-one years later, and now better known as Charles Kingsford-Smith, Charlie piloted the first aircraft to fly the Pacific Ocean. The sea did finally claim his life, however, when he crashed into the Indian Ocean in 1935. There have been thousands of rescues since young Smithy's, the most spectacular being on 'Black Sunday', 6 February 1938, when freak waves and a sandbank collapse swept 300 people out to sea. Luckily there were 70 lifesavers on the beach that day and all but five surfers were saved. Sharks are less of a problem, especially since regular offshore netting began—the only two recorded deaths here occurred in 1929, a fortnight apart.

The towered **Hotel Bondi** ❷ behind the beach—individually the most interesting building along Campbell Parade—opened as a first-class hotel in 1920, when Bondi was still mostly sandhills. Bondi Beach began gaining popularity as a picnic spot after its private owner opened it to the public in 1855. In 1882, when the owner sought assistance in controlling troublemakers, the government resumed the 10 hectares around the beach. The Bondi Baths opened in 1887, though daylight beach bathing was banned until 1902. By then the beach was a popular place to take in the sea air, especially after trams had reached the area in the 1890s.

In 1920 the beach had picnic areas, pine

trees, a bandstand, a raised tram turning area called 'the loop', and a twin-towered wooden pavilion, but by 1928 these had been replaced by the great waterfront promenades and the great loggia-fronted **Bondi Pavilion** ③. Promenading had become the go by the 1930s—day or night the pavilion was offering dancing and dancebands. With its 121-metre beach frontage, Bondi's Pavilion was on a grand scale, housing a ballroom, restaurant, cafe, gymnasium, Turkish bath, bars, open-air theatre, dressing sheds for 12 000 people and the surf-lifesaving club. Despite threats of drastic redevelopment, the pavilion continues as a fascinatingly multipurpose building. Look inside the central section to see photographic murals of Bondi Beach over the years.

At the southern end of the beach, climb the steps to Notts Avenue, near the Astra. Built as the fashionable Grand Hotel International in 1929 by Jack Shaw, a Jewish Russian emigre, the Astra had a palm court orchestra and roof garden. The Depression undermined it, though it struggled along with an increasingly seedy reputation before closing in 1983 and subsequently becoming retirement units.

Near the saltwater public baths, look back on the famous sweep of the beach with 1930s low-rise filling the northern ridge towards the Ben Buckler headland. On the rock shelf at the headland, a 240-tonne rock is easily seen. It was purportedly tossed up there by a storm in 1912. Beyond the ridge, the 1889 sewer vent 'chimney' rises at North Bondi. Above the pool, on Notts Avenue, the adjacent **Bondi Icebergs Club** ④ was formed in 1929 as Australia's first winter swimming club. Nowadays, the pool is showing its age, even if the members are not.

Towards the end of Notts Avenue the path drops to a concrete waterfront walk between rock overhangs and waves, crossing a gully called The Bight. It was probably here in 1809 that surveyor James Meehan bestowed the name 'Bundi Bay' on the area. Continue along the main path, climbing the headland at Mackenzies Point for sweeping views north and south—the south showing the way ahead to Bronte and the coastal slope of Waverley Cemetery.

Continue along below Marks Park and behind rocky Mackenzies Bay, up and around the next headland to Tamarama surf clubhouse. Below is the sandy expanse behind the narrow beach enclosed by cliffs, and backed by a neat park which continues across the road into steep-sided Tamarama gully. This area has had some radical facelifts. Until the 1880s, with its glens, ferns and waterfalls, this was Fletchers Glen, considered the most beautiful spot on the coast. It was redeveloped in 1887, when the tramway reached here, for the Bondi Aquarium, which featured swings, merry-go-rounds, razzle-dazzles, shooting galleries, Punch-and-Judy shows and a scenic railway. The aquarium burnt down and closed in 1891, but was replaced on an even greater scale in 1906 by **Wonderland City** ⑤. This predecessor to Luna Park had sideshows and stalls, underground rivers and cave rides, a large amusement building, an undulating roller-coaster snaking between the cliffs, even a mini-airship carrying passengers from clifftop to clifftop. Wonderland City did not survive long, closing about 1908.

Beach Couture

Daylight bathing was illegal before the turn of the century, but the rule was finally challenged and shattered at Manly Beach by a local newspaper editor. Thereafter, Bondi led the challenge to convention. Waverley Council made 'neck-to-knee' costumes for the beach compulsory in 1907, and prohibited sunbathing and 'mixing with the public' whilst in costumes—rules that were increasingly flouted. By the 1930s, huge crowds of male and female bathers were mixing on the beach on sunny days, most wearing almost identical dark one-piece costumes. Some men—controversially—had even begun baring their upper torsos!

Hollywood and World War II cracked the conservative fashion mould, but a desperate and well-publicised rearguard action was fought by Aub Laidlaw, beach inspector at Bondi for 30 years. Armed with a tape measure and Council authority to vet bikini sizes, he escorted offending girls off the beach, often amidst a blaze of publicity. The arrival of topless sunbathing briefly revived the debate and on Bondi, Sydney's first public beach to allow it, it was originally restricted to 'beyond the drain' at the southern end.

Bondi in the 1990s: sun, surfing and skin.

By then the beach was being called Tamarama, and gaining its own appeal. The surf club was established following a drowning in 1907.

Across the park, steps lead up to Tamarama Marine Drive which becomes Bronte Marine Drive at the next headland. From here Bronte Beach and Park spread out ahead. The local government area here is Waverley, which gets its name from Barnett Levey's 1824 'Waverley House', named in honour of Sir Walter Scott's

Waverley novels. The naming of Bronte also derives from a house, but without literary connections. 'Bronte House' was named by its second owner not after the literary sisters, but after Lord Nelson (created Duke of Bronte by the King of Sicily in 1798). The whole area was originally named Nelson Bay for the same reason, but that name is now restricted to the bay itself.

Further around, take the steps in front of the surf-lifesaving club down onto the concrete beach promenade. Bronte's beach is much smaller than Bondi's and the buildings less grand. But there is a thriving street cafe scene and Bronte's park is uncontested. More than 8 hectares of the original 23-hectare Bronte Estate are preserved in this fine gully, with picnic shelters, barbecues and playgrounds; there's even a miniature railway most weekends. There is a glorious variety of trees—Norfolk Island pines, Canary Island palms, figs, flame trees, gums and angophoras, banksias and bunya pines. Explore along the park's stone-lined creek where the valley narrows down between fig and flame trees. The valley head, where a waterfall cascades down to the stream, was known as Ebsworth Glen in the days when the Bronte Estate's ornamental gardens were here. The path climbs up through the former kitchen garden, vineyard and orchard and around to the left through the trees to the stables of 'Bronte House'.

A walk up onto Bronte Road leads to the Gothic two-storey stone lodge boldly marked **'Bronte'** ❻ and added in the 1860s by the house's third owner. The house rambles from the lodge through hallways to the turreted main building. A better look at Bronte House is possible from the split upper level of Bronte Road. Owned now by Waverley Council and leased as a private residence, it opens to the public several times a year. It was built by English barrister and politician, Robert Lowe, in 1846, on the then 42-acre (17-hectare) estate he had bought for £420. At least part of the house was designed by the Colonial Architect, Mortimer Lewis, with stables, outhouses, servants' cottages, cow-houses, pens and gardens added. Lowe returned to England after he had defended and lost in the controversial trial of a Captain Knatchbull who had been arrested literally red-handed for the murder and robbery of Mrs Ellen Jamieson. Lowe attempted an original defence, citing moral insanity, but Knatchbull went to the gallows nonetheless. Lowe's final act in the story was to adopt the murdered woman's two children and to take them home to England with him. Their new stepfather later became Viscount Sherbrooke, Chancellor of the British Exchequer and finally, Lord Sherbrooke. 'Bronte House' was so named by its next owner, J. J. Falconer, who bought the property in 1854. In the 1860s a third owner, J. B. Holdsworth, demolished at least one turret of the original house and added the many gothic touches, including the two-storey wing at the front.

Bronte Road leads back downhill to the cafes, beach, and the end of this walk where the options are to retrace your tracks or continue on to Walk 9.

Walk 9

Beaches 2
Bronte, Clovelly, Coogee

It is the succession of coastal inlets, cliffs and beaches south from Bondi—the invigorating and ever-changing interface of sea and land—that give these coastal walks their character and popularity. Beginning where the Bondi to Bronte Walk 8 left off, these two walks combine wonderfully.

Additional Reading
Randwick Municipal Council *Randwick: A Social History*, NSW University Press, 1985.

Background: Wylie's at Coogee—Sydney's finest heritage ocean baths

Features
Clifftop and beach scenery and structures
• seaside entertainments
• a superb cemetery
• sport and a mystery.

Distance
Approx. 5km (one way)
• links with Walk 8.

Time
1½ hours.

Difficulty
Easy to moderate
• steps and inclines
• generally unsuited to strollers and wheelchairs.

Access
Bronte, Clovelly and Coogee buses
• street parking.
UBD: Map 257 L9
Gregory's: Map 378 A9.

Facilities
Toilets and shops at Bronte, Clovelly and Coogee beaches • picnic spots throughout.

66 ✵ Sydney Strolls ✲ Eastern Suburbs

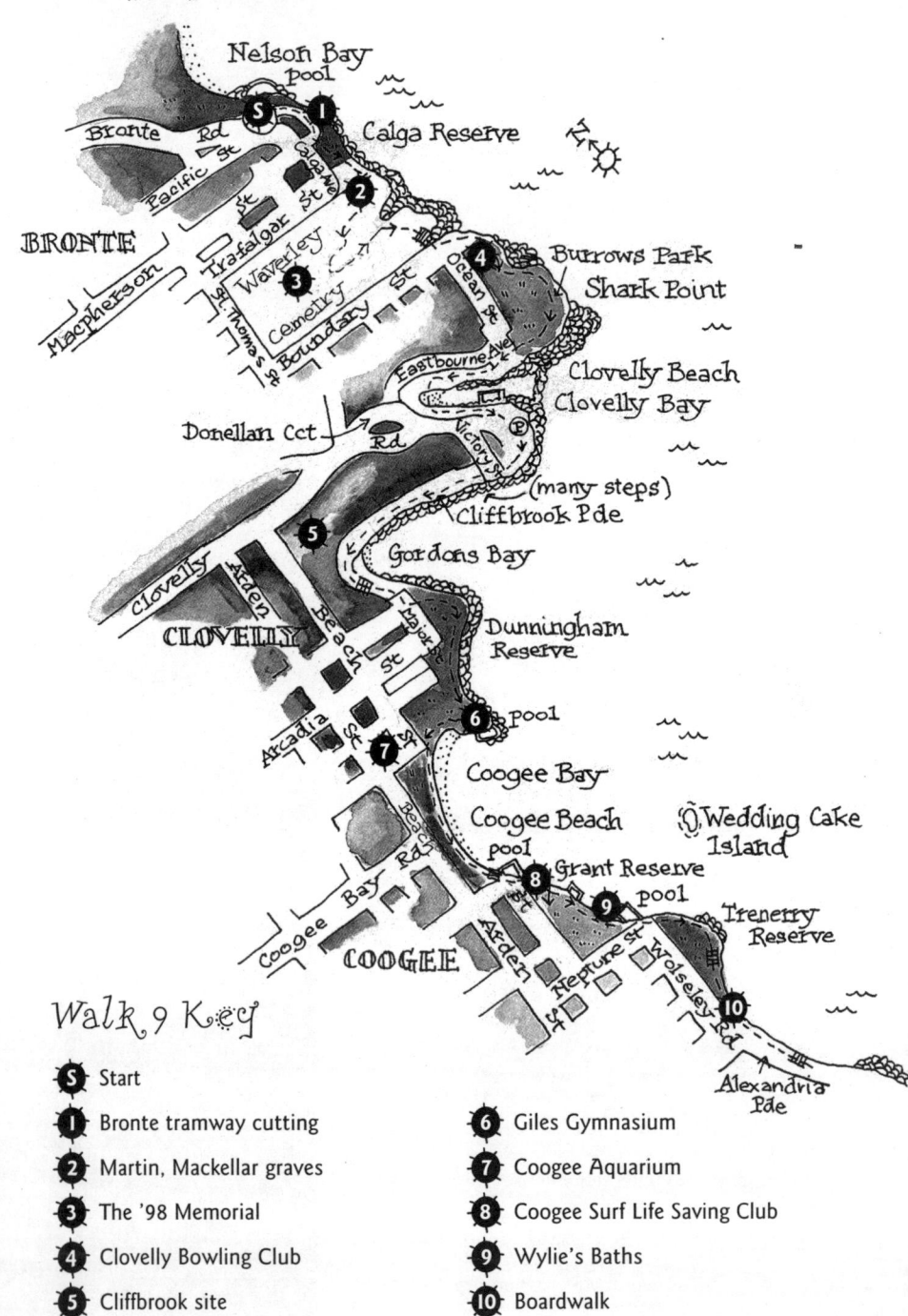

Walk 9 Key

- **S** Start
- **1** Bronte tramway cutting
- **2** Martin, Mackellar graves
- **3** The '98 Memorial
- **4** Clovelly Bowling Club
- **5** Cliffbrook site
- **6** Giles Gymnasium
- **7** Coogee Aquarium
- **8** Coogee Surf Life Saving Club
- **9** Wylie's Baths
- **10** Boardwalk

Bronte, Clovelly, Coogee ✹ **67**

Buses link to either end of this walk, so you can walk one way only or return. From Bronte Beach, the walk begins near the shops in the one-way road just above the beach. Follow this uphill through a **cutting** ❶ completed in 1911 and used by Bronte Beach trams until the end of the 1950s. Just before the former tramway reaches MacPherson Street, take the paved path across Calga Reserve along the cliffs towards Waverley Cemetery. This dramatically located cemetery, with its magnificent marble and granite memorials, opened in 1877 and reflects eastern suburbs social status. An extended wander is very rewarding but for now, just take a small diversion.

Where you entered the cemetery, a **'Grecian temple'** ❷ reflects the classical tastes of former NSW Premier Sir James Martin (see Walk 1, page 11). Immediately uphill from Martin, lie the Mackellars, notably Isobel Marion Dorothea Mackellar (see walks 2 and 3), poet of 'My Country'. Her grave seems a modest appendage to her family, including her wealthy and influential father, Sir (Dr) Charles Kinnard Mackellar.

Uphill on the same bitumen path, a prominent dome on the left commemorates Harry Rickards, the variety theatrical entrepreneur of Tivoli fame (see walk 2, page 18). Immediately uphill is a large Celtic cross at an intersection, memorialising New South Wales Governor Sir Robert William Duff who died in office in 1895. Now continue uphill and turn left at the next major T-junction, then right at the one after that. About 200 metres uphill, opposite the next T-intersection, is the spectacular **'98 Memorial** ❸. With its bronze revolutionary scenes, mosaics, wolf-hounds, axes, harps and serpents and other entwined Irish symbols, this memorial ostensibly commemorates Michael Dwyer, an elusive revolutionary leader from Wicklow south of Dublin, transported to Australia with other rebels from the 1798 rising in Ireland. In reality, it symbolises Ireland's long history of troubles and the 'Irish Cause' in Australia, a fact outlined by the newer memorials added at its rear.

There is so much more—Henry Lawson, Victor Trumper, Lawrence Hargrave—but for now turn back downhill and continue directly back to the waterfront. Three rows beyond the T-junction that you turned right from earlier, look in to the left for the distinctive headstone of Charles Peart, High Diving Champion of the World. Brought to Australia by Fitzgerald Brothers Circus, his final dive, at Redfern in 1896, was from a 14-metre tower into a 2.4- by 1.8-metre tank containing only a metre of water. It had worked before—this time it didn't. His headstone was provided by his grieving employers, some of whom are also buried here.

Back near the cliffs, resume the coastal walk across to and up the steps to Boundary Street. Ocean Street is the easiest way ahead, but an alternative is to follow the cliff path behind the **Clovelly Bowling Club** ❹ and around the rugged cliff face and cliff-top dam to the sandstone headland of Shark Point. A few remnants of another coastal gun position similar to ones once at the Signal Station (see walk 6, page 45) are to be found.

Nearest in the southward stretch of coast is Clovelly Bay. Originally called

The Case of the Shark's Arm

On 18 April 1935 a fisherman off Coogee Beach caught a small shark which, before he could haul it in, was devoured by a huge tiger shark, 4.5 metres long. Two for the price of one! As the fisherman's brother operated the Coogee Aquarium, the pair put the shark on display. On the Anzac Day weekend, with a large crowd of onlookers watching in amazement, the shark suddenly coughed up a human arm, setting off a bizarre murder investigation.

The arm had a tattoo of two boxers on it, as well as a rope around its wrist, and investigation showed it had been cut off its owner's body by a knife, not by the shark. Through fingerprints and the tattoo, the police identified the arm's owner as a former boxer and minor criminal named Jimmy Smith. Continued investigation suggested that Smith had been part of a drug-smuggling and insurance scam. 'Mr Big' appeared to be a wealthy Lavender Bay boatbuilder named Reginald Holmes, and his associate—who had apparently fed Jimmy in bite-sized chunks to the sharks—was a Patrick Brady. Holmes panicked and attempted suicide, then agreed to become a witness. However, hours before the inquest was to begin, Holmes was found in his car in Milsons Point—shot dead. With the main witness conveniently out of the way and the defence lawyers successfully arguing that an arm was not a body (and therefore no proof that a murder had even taken place), Brady walked free. The case remains unsolved.

The dome of the former Coogee Aquarium is still a prominent part of the landscape at the northern end of Coogee Beach.

Little Coogee, it was renamed after a picturesque Devon fishing village and does have something of a picture-postcard fishing harbour look. A breakwater tames the waves at the narrow entrance and beyond is a calm, narrow concrete-banked cove 350 metres long leading to a quiet little beach. There is an enclosed pool as well but the whole cove is a 'swimming pool', and one very popular for snorkelling. On the near horizon sits the imposing rear end of the Clovelly Hotel built in 1923 after the demolition of an 1859 castellated mansion called 'Mundarrah Towers'.

Follow the waterfront around across the beach to rejoin the path, and up past the kiosk and across the parking area. You can see Wedding Cake Island to the south, about 400 metres out to sea off Coogee. It is a small, flat rock outcrop that is an important fish-breeding area.

Take the footpath called Cliffbrook Parade alongside Gordons (or Thompsons, on some maps) Bay, the least spoiled inlet on this part of the coast. After some steep steps, the path drops towards the bay's head, which is usually covered by small boats on racks. The water is generally placid, almost tropical looking, and with the cliffs, quiet rock platforms, scrub and trees, this inlet has an unexpectedly secluded ambience—if the houses at the very top are ignored. There is an underwater nature trail here, though flippers and snorkels would seem a prerequisite for walking it.

Before its demolition in 1976 a large, rambling and splendidly adorned Victorian Mansion, **'Cliffbrook'** **5**, sat above the bay. It was built by John Thompson, Mayor of Randwick in 1873. An early 20th-century owner, Sir Denison Miller (first Governor of the Commonwealth Bank) sold the foreshore to the Council for the reserve and built an additional 'Cliffbrook House', still standing, which was for a time an Australian Atomic Energy Commission establishment. The path leaves the bay to climb to Major Street and Dunningham Reserve. A short walk through the heath out to the cliff face (noting the warning signs about unstable cliff faces) offers great views in most directions, including the bombora offshore favoured by board riders.

Back on the trail south, the headland rolls over to reveal Coogee with its beach, promenade, parks and busy shops and hotels fronting the beach. At about this point in March 1888, when daylight bathing was illegal but Coogee was a popular picnic spot, artists Tom Roberts and Charles Conder sat side by side to produce two of Sydney's earliest significant Impressionist paintings.

Coogee is particularly rich in bathing establishments and the buildings on this point were associated with **'Giles' Gymnasium'** **6** (originally men only), its 1920s structures including the now disused Turkish baths. Despite the meaning of its name (an Aboriginal word for 'stinking place', presumably referring to rotting seaweed), Coogee outshone Bondi as a beach centre until World War II, with picnics, horse racing on the sands, some hotels, early morning and late afternoon beach bathing, and private enclosed baths. Visitor numbers grew, especially after steam trams to here replaced horse-drawn omnibuses in 1883. By then there was a grand stone-walled promenade and wheeled wooden bathing machines to facilitate bathing in a modest age.

At the northern end of the beach stands an unusual white-domed building which opened in 1887 as the **Coogee Palace Aquarium and Pleasure Grounds** **7**. Along the lines of English seaside palaces, the grounds took up a whole block, combining fishtanks with dancing, toboggan rides, swimming baths, rollerskating, and picnic and children's play areas.

It was supplanted as an amusement centre in 1928 by a huge English-style Fun Pier built out into the sea. Here people promenaded, amused themselves at various games and entertainments or simply watched the surfers. Of an evening, thousands attended concerts and dances. Several hotels—none finer than the Georgian-style Tidwell's Hotel (now the Coogee Bay Hotel)—lined the streets, and Coogee's popularity increased with the installation of Sydney's first beach shark safety net in 1929. There was even floodlit night surfing and a night surf carnival in the 1930s.

Despite grabbing headlines in 1935 (see feature box, page 68), the Palace Aquarium closed soon after, becoming a picture theatre before almost rusting away. It survives, revived now in a multi-purpose role. The Fun Pier was severely damaged by storms in the 1930s and it and the shark net were removed during World War II. Today's promenade and amenities are post-1970s, a major revamp of the beachfront having been undertaken in the mid-1990s.

The **Coogee Surf Life Saving Club** **8**, at the southern end of the beach, was established in 1907, proving its worth with 300 rescues in its first two years. Below the club lies the 1947 Ross Jones Memorial Pool, a small tidal pool. A little further south, off Grants Reserve, the next saltwater pool is now unique. Built in 1872, the Ladies' and Children's Baths was single-sex from its beginning and remains so—having successfully defended itself in the 1990s in an anti-discrimination court case. Beyond it are the more spectacular **Wylie's Baths** **9**, opened in 1907 by champion swimmer, Henry Alexander Wylie. Taken over by the Council in 1978, the baths were superbly refurbished in 1994 and, with its long-legged amenities platform high above the water, Wylie's is Sydney's finest surviving early ocean pool. Henry's daughter, Wilhemina 'Mina' Wylie (1890–1984) trained here and at the Ladies' Baths along with Sarah 'Fanny' Durack (1889–1956). At the Stockholm Olympics in 1912, Fanny won the 100 metres while Mina took the freestyle silver, becoming the first Australian women Olympic medal winners.

The walk could end at Wylie's, where the choices are either the Coogee buses or a return walk to Clovelly or Bronte along the same route or through adjacent streets. However, much of Grant Reserve nearby has been beautifully developed into a series of tree-enclosed precincts well worth exploring. It and Trenerry Reserve lead also to a walking path continuing southwards along a marvellous **boardwalk** **10** crossing delicate coastal flora and rockfaces. At the moment, the track peters out into the streets of northern Maroubra, although the cliff walk can be found again and resumed around to Maroubra Beach for the very energetic.

Walk 10

Racing Through Randwick

Today's Randwick is understandably famous for horseracing, but its centre, a kilometre from the course, contains evidence of affluence, fine living, town planning and long-established civic pride. Some of this derives from the personal determination, political and financial influence of one man who wanted to reorder the world of his youth.

Additional Reading
Randwick: A Social History (Randwick Municipal Council), NSW University Press, 1985.
Simeon Pearce *Randwick: Dream and Reality* (Randwick Municipal Council), NSW University Press, 1990.

Background: St Judes Church seen through its 'English country churchyard'.

Features
Historic buildings, churchyard and people
• local politics
• industry.

Distance
Approx. 6km.

Time
2–2½ hours.

Difficulty
Mainly easy; some steps and inclines • generally suitable for strollers • wheelchair access to most points of interest.

Access
Randwick buses; backstreet parking.
UBD: Map 257 B15
Gregory's: Map 377 B15.

Facilities
Toilets, picnics at Alison Park • food shops, hotels throughout.

72 ※ Sydney Strolls ✲ Eastern Suburbs

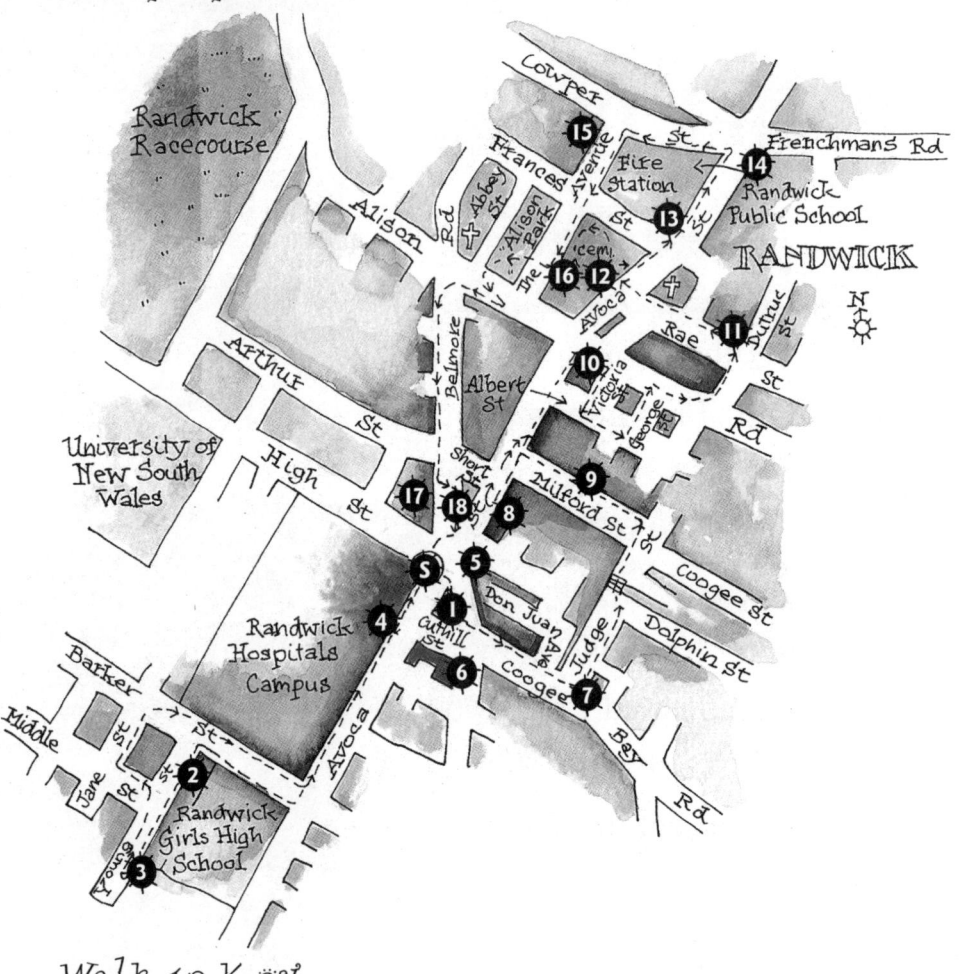

Walk 10 Key

- **S** Start
- **1** High Cross Park
- **2** 'Newmarket'
- **3** The 'Big Stable'
- **4** Former Destitute Children's Asylum
- **5** 'Corona' and 'Hygeia'
- **6** Royal Hotel
- **7** Randwick 'Lock-Up'
- **8** Our Lady of the Sacred Heart church
- **9** 'Nugal Hall'
- **10** Coach & Horses Hotel
- **11** 'Earlswood'
- **12** St Judes church and cemetery
- **13** Town Hall
- **14** 'Archina'
- **15** 'Tayar'
- **16** 'Avonmore'
- **17** 'Sandgate'
- **18** Former Star and Garter Inn

Amidst the sandy wastes two kilometres above Coogee Beach, Simeon Pearce (see feature box, page 75) set out to create an idealised New World version of the Gloucestershire Randwick that had failed him in his youth. His model village was never quite realised, but Pearce's vision left its mark.

The main walk begins near **High Cross Park** ❶, but there is a possible and highly interesting initial diversion, which begins south of the Randwick Hospitals Campus in Barker Street, near the Girls High School. Take a left turn into Young Street—a street of stables with a great Victorian house, **'Newmarket'** ❷, with courtyard and servants' wing, dominating the area like a manor house. At the street's far end is the **'Big Stable'** ❸, a great weatherboard building with a sky-lighted roof labelled 'Newmarket'. In the adjacent streets, especially Middle and Jane streets, are rows of tiny workers' cottages, older than the great house. This area, originally nicknamed 'Struggletown', began with 1850s cottages built by the ubiquitous Simeon Pearce for his workers and local craftsmen, near—but not too near—his ideal village.

In 1860 the Australian Jockey Club assumed control of Randwick Racecourse. Later, another course developed at Kensington where the University of New South Wales now is. Struggletown became the obvious location for horse sales and a community of strappers, jockeys, horse-handlers and trainers. A Newmarket Hotel—the name chosen, no doubt, to echo the famous English horse market town near Cambridge—was built by John Dillon in 1861 along with the Big Stable, and the racing fraternity moved in. Then, in 1918, William Inglis purchased the Big Stable and the hotel, turning the latter into the Inglis family home, 'Newmarket'. Big and little stables now belong to the Inglises, temporarily housing horses brought in from throughout Australia for regular sales in the modern glass-walled saleyard near the house. During World War II, though, the Big Stable had a different use—as a detention barracks for AWOL soldiers.

Once you've explored this unique area, return to Barker Street—named for the Anglican Bishop who established the first Bishop's official residence ('Bishopsgate', now demolished) nearby as a result of Simeon Pearce's efforts. Randwick Hospitals Campus, which now dominates this entire block, was preceded by another Pearce project seen after a left turn into Avoca Street. More than halfway up the block, the first large sandstone building is the Victorian Romanesque-style Catherine Hayes Block of the former **Destitute Children's Asylum** ❹. Social and economic change, poverty and childbirth mortality rates left hundreds of children homeless in mid-19th century Sydney. The philanthropic society attempting to house them was persuaded by Pearce to construct a new asylum at Randwick, built between 1856 and 1858. The Hayes block—named after an Irish opera singer who donated £800 towards its construction—was added in 1870 after 63 children had died in the overcrowded original building during a whooping cough epidemic. The next sandstone building is the original asylum block, designed in Regency style by Edmund Blacket, and next along again is a smaller building designed by J. Horbury Hunt in 1863 as the Superintendent's House. State welfare took over the asylum's functions and it closed in 1915, the buildings becoming a military hospital, and, subsequently, part of the Prince of Wales Hospital.

At High Street, cross Avoca Street to High Cross Park **1**. This crossroads, called High Cross in the English mode, was central to Pearce's village and retains a certain nobility despite traffic and modern buildings. Look around. Note the curious Church-like building due north with Captain Cook out front (more on both later). Also notice, the grand tower of a real church, the Sacred Heart. Colourful **'Randwick Lodge' 5** nearby is the latest incarnation of 'Corona' and 'Hygeia', an Italianate Victorian pair built in 1898. On High Cross Park itself, now with its war memorial, Pearce's volunteer Randwick Rifles militia once drilled. Beyond, in Cuthill Street, elegant in lovely filigree finery, is the 1887 **Royal Hotel 6** with some Victorian houses surviving nearby.

Cross to the northern side of Coogee Bay Road, moving towards the ocean. Opposite on the southern side of the road are the Brigidine Convent and College, established after 1901 in Edward Daintrey's 1859 home. On this side is 'Glen Mervyn', built in 1924 for meat supplier, Thomas Field, and donated to the Red Cross during World War II. Just across Judge Street is another girls' school, Claremont College, its corner building being the 1882 Randwick Police Station, still labelled **'Lock-Up' 7**. Turn left into Judge Street, taking the steps down, then continuing uphill and turning left into Milford Street.

About halfway along Milford, **Our Lady of the Sacred Heart church 8**, already seen from High Cross, is visible again on your left. Built in 1887 in a beautiful French provincial Gothic style, it was the first Catholic church in the Municipality. On the north side of Milford Street, Gothic **'Nugal Hall' 9**, with rusticated stone, gables and turrets, overlooks its modern neighbours. One of the first fine homes Pearce attracted to his village, 'Nugal Hall' was designed in the 1850s by architect Mortimer Lewis for merchant Alexander MacArthur and sat originally on a 22 acre (9 ha) estate. Cross the street to look into the charming remnant garden with its statuary and pump.

Almost at the head of the street on the right is another fine (though crowded) restoration, 'Milford House' (1879). Now a nursing home, it was once the residence of Sir John See, several times Mayor of Randwick and between 1901 and 1904, Premier of New South Wales. On the southern corner of Milford and Avoca is Georgian-style 'Ventnor', now church property, but originally the 1870s home of another Randwick Mayor, George Kiss, who owned the uninvitingly named 'Kiss Horse Bazaar' in Sydney. This might be a good time to divert southwards for a closer look at 'Ventnor' and the church, the fine interior of which includes stained glass windows from Tours, France.

Afterwards, retrace your steps to Milford then continue north along Avoca Street. Beyond the bold blue Marist centre are fine terraces and free-standing turn-of-the-century Italianate houses with names from the Devon seaside. At Alison Road, note the 1897 Federation Post Office

Randwick Revisited—Simeon Pearce

Simeon Pearce was born in Randwick, Gloucestershire, in 1821. Trapped socially between the newly poor and the newly prosperous of the Industrial Revolution, he faced a life as an agricultural worker. Aged 20, he chose instead to migrate to Australia where he decided to create a new Randwick—in which he would be amongst the prosperous. Clever, industrious, successful—and profitably married—in the 1840s he bought up most of the sandy waste that became central Randwick. He began promoting his new Randwick cleverly as a location for superior coastal estates for the elite. The first was his own, 'Blenheim', named after a mansion in the English Randwick. He even conducted local fox hunts for leading citizens, including the Governor.

Using his political and judicial connections, Pearce achieved municipal status for Randwick in 1859, rigging the boroughs to ensure that he became Mayor. His frustrated enemies, led by John Moore (of Moore Park), bided their time. Mayor five times in the municipality's first 10 years, Pearce was eventually rolled by his enemies, although he managed one last term in 1882. Pearce's elegant, idealised Randwick was soon inundated by suburbanisation. The trams arrived in 1880 and the municipality's population passed 6000 soon after Pearce's death in 1886. Twenty-five years later the population reached 35 000—few of whom had ever heard of Simeon Pearce.

The original Blacket-designed block of the former Destitute Children's Asylum. One of Simeon Pearce's great achievements was to bring the Asylum to his Randwick.

across the road, but turn right at the 1856 **Coach and Horses** ⑩, Randwick's first hotel. Take the next right into Victoria Street, where numbers 8 and 10 (built in the 1880s by another Mayor, George Denning) present an interesting comparison, their old stables visible at the rear. At street's end, turn left down Albert Street with the ocean ahead and 'Nugal Hall' glimpsed again on your right. Take the next left into George Street, past attractive, stone cottages at numbers 8 and 6, and then turn right into Alison again. A hundred metres or so downhill, cross over to Dutruc Street and climb to Rae Street. On the north-west corner of the intersection is the gloriously High Victorian **'Earlswood'** ⑪, with its wealth of detailing and decoration and the date below the female bust under the pediments. Turn left up Rae Street to find large Victorian terraces (1887) followed by Federation terraces and an 1883 Wesleyan chapel.

Cross Avoca Street to the marvellous **St Jude's precinct** ⑫ amidst its English trees. The story of St Judes—named for the saint of 'hope for the hopeless'— encapsulates much of the Simeon Pearce story. Seeking a reproduction of the St John's church of his native Randwick, Pearce provided the land, but money was needed. When a former resident bequeathed money to build a church at 'Big Coogee', Pearce convinced the executors that this meant Randwick. Edmund Blacket was commissioned to design the church and construction began in 1861. But when Pearce's rival Charles Moore and his fellow-Coogeeans realised what was happening, they took legal action and stalled construction. However, Moore's strong legal argument was no match for Pearce's excellent judicial connections— the court ruled in Pearce's favour in 1864 and by 1865 Pearce had his village church. Later additions (the 1877 clocktower and 1888 transept) altered its appearance somewhat. The rectory next door was added in 1870.

Behind the church, St Jude's cemetery is the eastern suburbs' only English-style churchyard. The well-spaced tombstones of the wealthy early Anglican congregation give the illusion of edging serenely onto fields and forest. Small and easily explored, the gravestones of Pearce, Archibald Mosman (after whom the North Shore suburb is named), Ann Hordern (wife of Anthony Hordern) and others of interest can be found.

Return to Avoca Street and continue north past the last building in the St Jude's group to the Frances Street corner where a delightfully proportioned 1867 French provincial-style structure is now the Parish Centre. It was built as Pearce's first Borough Chambers, and across Frances Street is the later **Town Hall** ⑬, an impressive Victorian Classical civic statement also commissioned by Pearce, in 1881. The original building (1886) of Randwick Public School is next door.

Further north, at the corner of Cowper Street, look across Avoca Street to the Frenchmans Road corner where 'Archina' ⑭ (1907) stands. Behind 'Archina', in Chapel Street, is another house, 'Ascot' (1888). The two were part of a site of pioneering and controversial industrial significance. The Sacred Heart missionaries purchased 'Ascot' in 1907, and their

Procurator, Father Shaw, a pioneer of radio, established the Maritime Wireless Company on the site to help fund missionary activities. The factory buildings (demolished in 1998) incorporated an extensive radio manufacturing plant with a distinctive 55-metre aerial. The property was purchased at a suspiciously high price in 1915 by the navy for munitions manufacture. Shaw, it seems, had misappropriated mission funds and made generous monetary gifts to the Minister for the Navy and a Tasmanian Senator. Both politicians were forced to resign, and soon afterwards, Father Shaw was found dead in a hotel room in circumstances never explained. From 1924, the factory was used by Wing Commander Lawrence Wackett as the RAAF experimental station. Here the talented Wackett designed five aircraft including the successful Widgeon amphibians which went into RAAF service. Despite its success, the government closed the plant in 1930 during the Depression (after pressure from English aircraft manufacturers). Wackett quit the air force but during World War II re-emerged as Managing Director and chief designer at the Commonwealth Aircraft Corporation.

Turn left off Avoca at Cowper and continue past Randwick Primary School. Across the street is the 1900 mansion **'Tayar'** 15, while 'Peckham' (1886) perches on the western corner as you turn into The Avenue. Beyond the impressive 1908 Federation-style Fire Station, The Avenue leads verdantly between St Jude's cemetery and Alison Park to **'Avonmore'** 16, an 1888 terrace which could be one of Sydney's finest with some judicious restoration. Facing the park across Alison Street, some fine 1890s houses, now part of Marcellan College, nestle amidst the trees. Further west, shopfronts and demolitions have undone a once elegant row of houses. At the corner of Belmore Road look across to the classically elegant facade of the Presbyterian church designed in 1885 by Sir John Sulman.

Belmore Road, the main shopping street, is lively and multicultural. There is an old shopfront at number 126, and next door is **'Sandgate'** 17, an 1871 survivor, currently a restaurant. On the Short Street corner opposite stands the building which was Randwick's first post office (1878–98). Further along, on High Cross junction, is a building whose styles are as mixed as its history. The back part began as the **Star and Garter Inn** 18 in the 1850s, then became a school. In 1869 Captain Thomas Watson (formerly of 'Clovelly' at Watsons Bay—see Walk 7, page 52) purchased it, adding the tower to see the sea, as well as the Captain Cook statue out front to celebrate the 1870 centenary of Cook's exploration. The building later became a school again and then, from the 1890s to 1987, was Hannans' butcher shop.

The walk ends here at High Cross, although if you need to return to Barker Street, a short stroll remains.

Walk 11

Homes & Gardens
Daceyville

Features
Significant, historic and charming public housing project.

Distance
Approx. 3km.

Time
1½ hours.

Difficulty
Easy • stroller and wheelchair accessible.

Access
Anzac Parade buses to southern end of Kingsford shops • street parking.
UBD: Map 276 M2
Gregory's: Map 406 G2.

Facilities
Picnic spots at Daceyville Reserve and Astrolabe Park
• Kingsford shops.

Dacey Gardens is possibly Sydney's most significant and attractive historic example of public planning and housing. It was Sydney's first public housing experiment; its first government-planned garden suburb; its first expression of the Californian bungalow; and even its first planned cul-de-sac.

Additional Reading
Graeme Butler *The California Bungalow in Australia*, Lothian, 1992.
Max Kelly *Sydney: City of Suburbs*, NSW University Press, 1987.

Background: The Dacey Gardens style, garden-set flats built in Cook Avenue, 1915.

Late in the 19th century, town planners such as Ebenezer Howard reacted to the cramped, unhygienic and ill-serviced jerry-built terraces that the Industrial Revolution had thrown across English and European landscapes. The concept of the well-planned 'garden city', and its lesser form, the 'garden suburb', developed and spread. In Sydney, Haberfield was one of the garden suburb movement's first expressions, developed by Richard Stanton from 1901.

In 1909 the first of several Royal Commissions on the improvement of Sydney recommended future planning directions, and in 1912, the New South Wales Labor Government Treasurer, John Rowland Dacey, unveiled a proposal for a 336-acre (137-hectare) working man's garden suburb. Dacey died within weeks of the announcement and the development was named after him. Architect–planners Sir John Sulman and J. F. Henessey prepared an innovative tree-lined, unfenced, garden-set layout fanning out between Bunnerong and Gardeners roads. It would be a self-contained suburb with schools, shops, community hall, churches, baby health centre and a police station. A 1912 competition seeking compatible housing designs was won by S. G. Thorpe, whose partner, James Peddle, had been working in Pasadena, California. There he had been impressed by the bungalow designs that the Greene Brothers were introducing and his ideas were picked up by his Sydney partner. Other designs were provided by the Government Architect and the Housing Board—through its architect William Foggitt. World War I intervened, slowing construction and changing the theme of street names from explorers to notable wartime figures.

While construction continued after the war, the great plan was never completed. Governments and priorities changed and only about 300 of the proposed thousands of dwellings were complete by 1924, after which the remaining development was privatised. However, the Dacey Gardens houses remained in public hands, controlled after World War II by the new Housing Commission and, later, by its successor, the Department of Housing. In the 1980s the area's heritage value was recognised in an imaginative program of restoration mixed with sympathetic infill housing. Much of Dacey Gardens is now of 1980s origin or reconstruction, but the outcome is true to the estate's original feel—it is often difficult to tell old from new. Homes and units sit individually or clustered on open, unfenced blocks amidst superb trees and gardens. Under iron and tile roofs, textures of brick, timber and stucco mix with ochres, fawns, brick-reds, deep pinks, muted greens, blues and greys, creating a great sense of integrity while allowing a certain individuality. Dacey Gardens remains an innovative and inviting showpiece of public housing.

The walk begins at the columned entrance to Daceyville Reserve just beyond Kingsford's Nine Ways, with the suburb's major roads fanning out ahead. The attractive large central building with a lantern-like dome, **'Foggitt House'** ❶, dominates General Bridges Crescent beyond the reserve and sets the little suburb's tone. These impressive 1980s flats occupy the site of the 1917 Daceyville Public Hall, destroyed by fire in 1985. Towards

80 ❋ Sydney Strolls ⚓ Eastern Suburbs

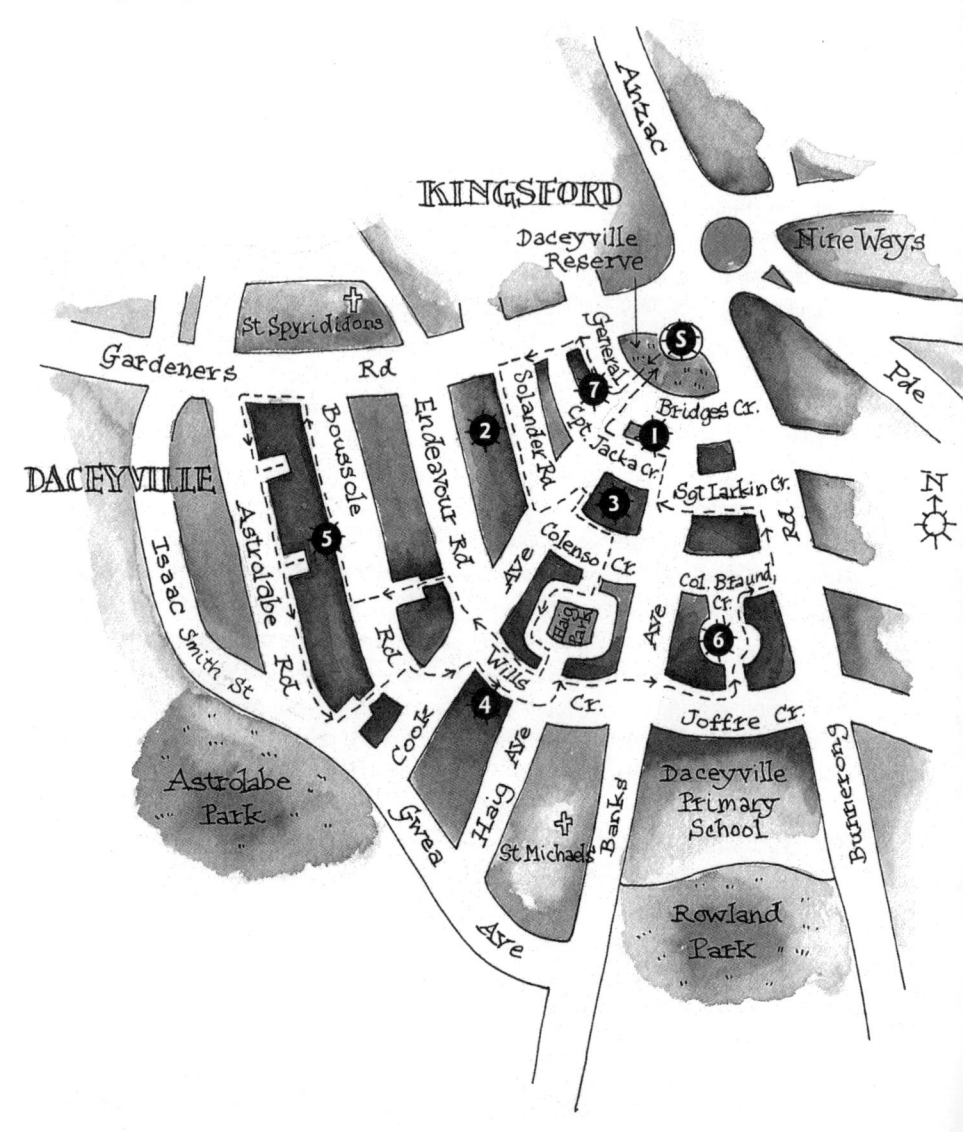

Walk 11 Key

- **S** Start
- **1** Foggitt House
- **2** 1–7 Solander St
- **3** 2–8 Cook Ave
- **4** Former baby health centre
- **5** 13–23 Boussole Rd
- **6** Colonel Braund Crescent cul-de-sac
- **7** Police Station

Gardeners Road, at numbers 1–11, are the only shops built on the estate, all with residences above. In 1917 they housed a grocer, a bootmaker, a draper, a greengrocer and a fancy goods store. The adjacent Kingsford shops have undermined their role, but not their style. The crescent itself is named after Major-General Sir William Bridges, creator of the first AIF, who insisted that the Australian forces maintain a separate identity and not be integrated into the British Army. Bridges was killed at Gallipoli in 1915 and is buried at Duntroon, the army college in Canberra.

Turn left into Gardeners Road and note numbers 19–21, a very typical pair of essentially Federation semis, designed in 1913 by the Government Architect. Around the corner, in Solander Street, is some of the variety now typical of the estate. **Numbers 1–7** ❷, sets of semis, are in the winning 1913 design of S. G. Thorpe. Linking a two-storey gabled dwelling with a single-storey one, and using the Californian look, were unusual ideas. Numbers 9–11 demonstrate a feature of the 1980s renovation of the estate—backlots infilled with sympathetic designs—in this case units for the elderly.

Follow Solander down to Cook Avenue and note how the angled corner buildings contribute to the comfortable openness of the streetscape. Across the road, **numbers 2–8 Cook Avenue** ❸ are the first of another distinctive design—a well-proportioned block of four flats built in 1915 with a large centre gable and arched entrance to their backyard. Cross over to Colenso Crescent (once Burke Crescent and renamed after a local resident in 1961) where this design is repeated.

Cook Avenue is named after Captain James Cook, who arrived in Botany Bay aboard his ship *Endeavour* in April 1770. First to jump ashore from the Captain's cutter was teenager Isaac Smith, cousin to Cook's wife. Cook's scientific expedition included a Swedish naturalist, Dr Daniel Solander, and a young, wealthy scientist, Joseph (later Sir Joseph) Banks. It was Banks in particular who later helped convince the British Government—looking for somewhere to deposit their surplus convicts after losing the American War of Independence—to proclaim New South Wales a British colony and send the first fleet to settle Botany Bay.

Upon their arrival in Botany Bay, the new Governor, Captain Arthur Phillip, and his officers, immediately realised that the bay area did not match up to Banks's vision as a suitable place for settlement. Fortunately for them their explorations revealed the magnificent harbour of Port Jackson, which Cook had not investigated, and the settlement was made there. Remarkably, only six days after the fleet's arrival in Botany Bay, two more ships turned up—*L'Astrolabe* and *La Boussole*—a French scientific expedition under the command of Comte de Lapérouse (see Walk 13, page 91). After a stay of several friendly weeks, the French expedition sailed off into the Pacific and was lost with all hands in the Santa Cruz Islands. Cook, Banks, Solander, Isaac Smith and the ships *Endeavour*, *L'Astrolabe* and *La Boussole* are all commemorated in street names, and are visible along this walk.

Opposite the larger 1915 blocks in Colenso Crescent, are some smaller cottages. A path between the symmetrical

Bungalow Building

Between the wars Sydney was swept by bungalow building—raw suburbs of liver-coloured brick houses, nestling under gables and high-pitched red-tiled roofs. This was the new peoples' housing, democratic in feel, and modest in cost, appearance and maintenance. Bungalows on their quarter-acre blocks matched post-World War I family lifestyles. The style lost favour after World War II and many disappeared beneath unsympathetic renovations, before more recently recovering some popularity. Kingsford and Rosebery (intended as a garden suburb) offer many examples nearby.

Usually called 'Californian' bungalows, they were really Sydney bungalows. The Californian style, as it evolved in Pasadena from the domestic architecture of the Greene Brothers, had a more organic quality. Rough stonework, clinker bricks, stucco and stained or deep natural-coloured timbers reflected nature. The low-pitched roofs in bitumened metal or redwood shingles overhung gables, rafters and cool sleep-out verandahs, often with tapered pillars.

Bungalow living was promoted as part of a healthy, natural lifestyle—homes which belonged to their natural environment. The similar Californian climate and lifestyle and the new admiration for Hollywood were also used to promote the bungalow style in Australia. Dacey Gardens estate began before the Australian style evolved and is a hybrid of the Californian and the established Federation style—the first step in the evolution of the Australian version of the Californian bungalow.

Shadows and streetscape link the cottages of Sergeant Larkin Crescent, Dacey Gardens.

numbers 5 and 7 leads into Haig Park, its central oval a satisfying space circled by an access road. The park and nearby street are named after Field Marshal Douglas Haig, Commander-in-Chief of the British (and therefore Australian) forces in France in World War I and whose generalship filled war cemeteries throughout north-west France. The through-path emerges into Wills Street, named after the explorer, William Wills, who was co-leader with Robert O'Hara Burke (after whom Colenso Street was originally named) of the infamous 1860–61 expedition across Australia. Both of the explorers died at Coopers Creek. Opposite is St Michael's Catholic church (1921) and school, the only church built on the estate before the project fizzled out. On the south-west corner of the intersection of Wills and Haig streets, the former 1919 **Baby Health Centre** ❹ has suitably aged to become pensioner housing. Walk west along Wills to Cook Avenue and cross to Endeavour Road, noting the 1915 block angled on the corner. In the distance, across Gardeners Road, the facade of St Spryridon's Greek Orthodox church adds an exotic touch. Kingsford is home to a substantial Greek community, with many inhabitants originally from the tiny and remote island of Castellorizo.

Endeavour Road is another enticing street, but turn left up the lane between numbers 25 and 23 which opens into another small park. Each of these central public spaces has its own character, enhanced by playgrounds or street furniture, trellises and gardens. The townhouses are, again, infill but the result is impressive. Follow the roadway out to Boussole Road, emerging opposite another substantial infill—pensioner housing again. Turn to the right and follow Boussole along to Gardeners Road, noting the attractively set retirement units on the right and the 1914 Federation semis, **numbers 13–23 Boussole** ❺, designed by Foggitt. These are followed by larger, gabled semis (designed about the same time by the Government Architect) which continue around into Gardeners Road.

From Gardeners Road turn left into Astrolabe Road, where the two sides of the road are very different. The communal, compatible styles continue on the left, while the right has front fences and a jangling diversity of designs and colours. The public housing project stopped here, on the left. Most of this public housing is now rehabilitated or new, with three distinctive cul-de-sacs of infill housing worth investigating. At the bend in the road, Isaac Smith Street enters from the left against the apparently infinite greenness of Astrolabe Park—an illusion created by the adjacent golf courses. Take the cul-de-sac left signposted to numbers 58–64 Astrolabe, through the central public space and on to Boussole Road again. Turn right here and then left into Cook Avenue, cross over into Wills Street again, past St Michaels, and walk through to Banks Avenue.

Cross elegant Banks Avenue, with its central palms, to Joffre Crescent, named after Field-Marshal Haig's French equivalent in the first three years of World War I, and inspect Daceyville Primary School on the right, its substantial 1921 buildings reflecting the estate style. Just beyond the level crossing, take the footpath left and through into another **cul-de-sac** ❻.

Here a group of fine Californian bungalows heads up an interesting variety of buildings—mostly rehabilitated public housing, but with a few privately owned homes. This cul-de-sac, an extension of Colonel Braund Crescent, and was the first ever planned in Australia. This and the next crescent, Larkin, are named after serving members of the New South Wales Legislative Assembly killed at Gallipoli in 1915. Lieutenant-Colonel George Braund, Liberal Party Member for Armidale was killed in May; while Sergeant Edward Larkin, Labor Member for Willoughby, died a month later.

Turn right at Colonel Braund Crescent to Bunnerong Road where the bland brick 1950s blocks on the eastern side of the road contrast with the charm of Dacey Gardens estate. Turn left again into Sergeant Larkin Crescent where the simple Foggitt cottages end with two clearly privatised homes behind some uninspired 1950s brick apartments.

Cross Banks Avenue again, with its Phoenix palms, to Captain Jacka Crescent, a last charming street at the back of 'Foggitt House'. Albert Jacka was Australia's best-known World War I hero, winning, at Gallipoli, the first Australian Victoria Cross of the war. Jacka spurned opportunities for safer jobs and, apart from periods of hospitalisation recovering from wounds, spent the entire war in the front line where he also won a Military Cross and Bar in France for his extraordinary valour.

Turn right into Cook Avenue, past the 1920 **Police Station** ❼, and Daceyville Park and walk's end are just ahead.

Walk 12

Dangerous Coast

Little Bay, Cape Banks

The most dangerous things about this walk nowadays are probably golfers and traffic. The walk juxtaposes a sense of abandonment and nature's power with golf buggies on manicured courses. It has rare flora, shipwrecks, coastal defences and a lonely cemetery.

Additional Reading

Jack Loney *Wrecks on the New South Wales Coast*, Oceans Enterprises, 1993.

R. K. Fullford *We Stood and Waited: Sydney's Anti-Ship Defences 1939–1945*, Royal Australian Artillery Historical Society, 1994.

Background: Signs from a dangerous coast: Chinese seaman's gravestone with wartime observation post beyond.

Features
Coastal flora • clifftop and coastal scenery • historic military sites • shipwrecks • historic cemetery • golf courses.

Distance
Approx. 6km • links with Walk 13.

Time
2–3 hours.

Difficulty
Moderate • rocks, some damp areas • a torch is optional • only Jennifer Street Lands is suitable for stroller or wheelchair.

Access
Anzac Parade/La Perouse buses • street parking.
UBD: Map 297 B13
Gregory's: Map 437 B13.

Facilities
Nearest toilets and shops at La Perouse. No dogs in national park.

86 ✳ Sydney Strolls ⚓ Eastern Suburbs

Walk 12 Key

- **S** Start
- **1** Jennifer Street Lands boardwalk
- **2** Defence Department houses
- **3** No. 2 gun, Banks Battery
- **4** No. 1 gun, Banks Battery
- **5** Battery observation post
- **6** *Minmi* wreck
- **7** Henry Head fortifications
- **8** Large observation post
- **9** National parks workshop

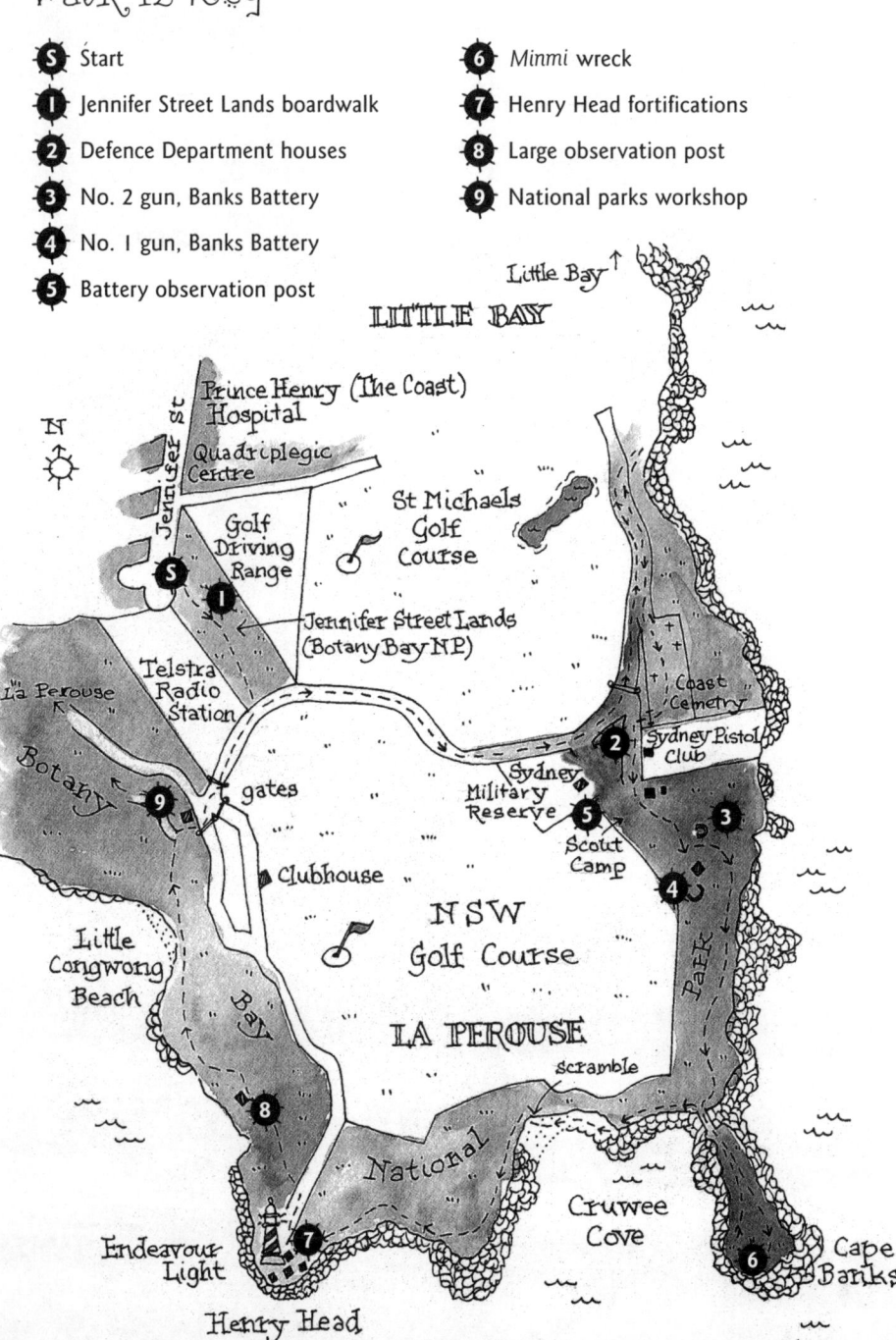

The walk begins at Botany Bay National Park's Jennifer Street Lands, 500 metres along Jennifer Street from Anzac Parade, immediately south of Prince Henry (The Coast) Hospital, Little Bay. Walk 12 links with Walk 13 at Henry Head and the two can easily be combined.

The tiny Jennifer Street Lands contain virtually the only surviving patch of the huge banksia shrubland which once covered most of the coast from Botany Bay to Centennial Park. Take the superb **boardwalk** ❶, opened in 1998, which slips 350 metres across the little forest, offering an environmentally responsible way to enjoy its atmosphere. The boardwalk and the Lands end at a bitumen road. Turn left and follow this road coastwards between the greens and fairways of St Michael's Golf Course, taking care to avoid motorists and stray golf balls. The St Michaels course was completed in 1939 on land that was formerly part of the Coast Hospital. Continue on until a small settlement of **Defence Department houses** ❷ is reached. As the bitumen road bends right and slightly uphill, continue more or less straight ahead past the gate on the signposted 'Coast Cemetery Management Trail'.

A hundred metres further on, the cobbled road opens into a turning circle outside the old Coast Cemetery. Continue north, for the moment, along the track between the golf course and the strip of coastal heath. Stop where there is a good view towards Little Bay and the coast beyond. Beyond the golfers is the back of Prince Henry Hospital, and it and the bay have been the site of sad and curious events. An isolation camp for victims of a smallpox epidemic was established at Little Bay in 1881 and from this developed the Coast Hospital. Thereafter victims of other infectious diseases such as typhoid, leprosy, bubonic plague, the post-World War I influenza epidemic, and even measles, whooping cough and diphtheria, were sent to the Coast over several decades. The hospital had isolation wards and self-contained lazarets (for lepers), but as medical advances overcame most infectious diseases, the need for a specialised hospital declined. In a sad parallel decades earlier, nearby Long Bay had a large cave known locally as the 'Blacks' Hospital' where the local Aboriginal people, devastated by smallpox, came together to die. In 1934 the Coast Hospital became Prince Henry, now a teaching hospital associated with the University of New South Wales.

Also visible beyond Long Bay are the remnants of some of the World War II observation posts and gunsites which once peppered this coastline. Visible, too, is the Belgian-built experimental wind generator placed above Long Bay in 1986. There is no evidence left, however, of what was possibly the oddest event to happen in the area. In late 1969, Bulgarian-born sculptural artist Christo (with about 125 assistants) wrapped part of Little Bay and its cliffs in 93 000 square metres of fabric using 56 kilometres of rope. The wrapping was removed (with wind assistance) after 10 weeks.

Turn back now for a visit to the cemetery. It is well maintained and despite the drifting conversation of the golfers and the proximity of the Defence Department buildings, seems the loneliest cemetery in Sydney. It is not hard to imagine how isolated it was at the turn of the century when small processions from the Coast Hospital, carrying those who died of infectious diseases, wound their way out here. The silent inscriptions of the scattered stones, including a couple with Chinese characters, speak quite volubly amidst the whispers of the ocean and the eternal golfers. You may also hear a more intrusive sound. Walk to the south-west corner of the cemetery and take the tiny path cutting up to the bitumen road near the houses. Immediately on the left is a pistol shooting range, little brother to the large Anzac Rifle Range back between Malabar and Maroubra—the warning signs should be observed. Further on there is evidence of bigger guns.

Enter the Cape Banks Scout Camp. The first buildings encountered are a toilet block and a locked anonymous military building that conceals a tunnel into a large underground engine room. Two clusters of concrete fortifications stand further afield. This was Banks Battery, a key part of Sydney's World War II seaward defences. At the nearest cluster it is possible to peek into an access shaft and the aboveground store rooms of what was **No. 2 gun** ❸. Steps lead to the roof and gun emplacement parapet where, remarkably, some of the camouflage paint is still visible. The gun floor has been destroyed along with the shell hoist shaft which lifted the shells from the magazines underneath. The further complex—**No. 1 gun** ❹, to the right across the camping ground—is similar. From its parapet, Cape Banks and the entrance into Botany Bay can be seen a few hundred metres south. The underground magazine chambers of this complex are accessible from the entrenched bunkers closest to the camping ground. Explorers will need a torch and should proceed with caution. The open bunkers by the tunnel entrance were the first aid post.

Banks Battery was built between 1935 and 1939. It consisted of two 9.2-inch guns which could fire 172-kilogram shells up to 26 kilometres every 20 seconds. Each gun and mounting weighed over 140 tonnes. The complex included the engine room, radar, searchlights and generators, barracks (the Defence Department housing came later) and anti-aircraft guns. The **Battery Observation Post and Plotting Room** ❺ can be seen on the hilltop back towards the Commonwealth houses. Like the entire site it was thoroughly camouflaged during World War II. There are more underground complexes in the hill behind the observation post. A similar battery to the one at Banks was located at North Head and, together with at least five batteries of smaller-calibre guns and five additional Fortress Observation Posts, they made up the interlocking 'Fortress Sydney', spread between Brookvale and Cape Solander. All were coordinated from a three-storey Fire Command Post at Dover Heights disguised to look like a block of red-brick flats. These coastal artillery units were finally disbanded around 1962 and the big guns sold for scrap.

From between the two gun emplacements, take the track down through the dunes (much overgrown by bitou bush, an unwelcome South African) towards the rocky headland of Cape Banks. Although virtually an island, Cape Banks is easily

Shipwrecked!

A maritime city is bound to have shipwreck stories (see Walk 7), and the coastline from Maroubra to Botany Bay has more than its share. The most commemorated was the Burns Philp Motor Vessel *Malabar*, 4602 tonnes, which ran aground in Long Bay on 2 April 1931. There were no fatalities but the ship broke up after two days, sending its cargo of tinned and packaged food ashore to the delight and benefit of the locals, who—perhaps in gratitude—renamed their village Malabar. In 1955 another large ship, the *Goolgwai*, came to grief at almost the same spot before disappearing into deeper water with the loss only of the ship's dog, 'Sluggo'.

A little further to the north, three ships came ashore around Maroubra Beach and headland—the 1530-tonne sailing ship *Hereward* in 1858 (a year in which 22 ships sank off the New South Wales coast); the 2488-tonne SS *Tekapo*, in 1859; and the *Belbowrie*, a 214-tonne wooden coastal steamer, in 1939. There were a dozen or more wrecks around Botany Bay heads. Only one of the 15 crew of the collier *Woniora* made it into Botany Bay when the ship rolled in heavy seas in 1882. In 1886, two lives and the steamer *Prince of Wales* were lost when the ship collided with SS *Peterborough* north-east of Botany Bay heads. In 1862, SS *Wonga Wonga* had run down and sunk the brigantine *Viceroy* in the same location. The rocks now occupied by the *Minmi*, on Cape Banks, also trapped the ketch *Sea Breeze* in 1883; two '*Pioneers*' and two '*Advances*' were lost here—and the list goes on.

A freighter entering Botany Bay passes Cape Banks with the remains of wreck of the Minmi, wrecked there in 1937, showing in the foreground.

accessed by the golf bridge (part of the New South Wales Golf Course) across to its northern lip. It has all the drama of an island bulwark against the ocean and, subject to sea and weather conditions, is well worth exploring. The power of the sea is graphically demonstrated by the 60-year-old **shipwreck** ❻ lying on the bay side of the headland—a rusty reminder of the many wrecks along this coast (see feature box, page 89). The 1484-tonne collier, *Minmi,* cracked her back on these rocks on 13 May 1937, with the loss of two of her 24 crew. The rest escaped by scrambling onto the rocks or along a rocket line fired from ship to shore. The survivors found shelter at the artillery garrison.

The first part of the track from here to Henry Head is less obvious than the earlier section of the walk. It begins with a walk, either partly along the edge of the golf course or along the rock shelves of Cruwee Cove, to the small beach at the cove's western end. Water is usually draining off the low heath and wetland over the rocky shelves and these should be crossed with care. A little more fancy footwork is needed after the small beach is crossed. The minimal track scrambles briefly up a tiny marshy creek at the end of the beach, reverses left over a plank and then improves as it climbs through taller heath.

It opens onto an elevated rock platform with good bay views, and the Endeavour Light, the small lighthouse at Henry Head, can be seen on the hillside just above. Take the wide track leading up to it from the far end of the rock shelf, and on around to the lighthouse and the **Henry Head fortifications** ❼. For more information on Henry Head see Walk 13.

From Henry Head much of the return to Jennifer Street Lands follows the same route as part of Walk 13. From the lighthouse and gun emplacements at Henry Head, follow the bitumen road away from the coast before branching left along the marked walking track uphill to the large military **observation post** ❽.

If Jennifer Street is the objective, continue 300 metres until the rear of the **national parks workshop** ❾ is reached. Follow the workshop's fence line to the roadway at the junction of the New South Wales Golf Club entrance and exit roads. With the club gates on your right, follow the public road through a road barrier towards St Michael's Golf Club. The boardwalk back through the Jennifer Street Lands to the end of the walk is about 200 metres beyond the barrier. If you prefer to continue along Walk 13 to La Perouse instead, follow the track past the rear of the national parks workshop towards Congwong Bay Beach.

Walk 13

inside Henry's Head

La Perouse, Botany Bay National Park

Europeans began visiting La Perouse, home to Aboriginal people for thousands of years, in 1770. They initially rejected it as unsuitable for settlement, and it seemed destined to be a place of outcasts. Now, although on the outer edge of the eastern suburbs, there is a sense of holiday in just being there.

Additional Reading
Sydney: City of Suburbs Max Kelly (Editor), NSW University Press, 1987.

Background: Across the bridge to Bear Island, La Perouse's futile but fascinating fort.

Features
Historic and military sites and buildings; bushland and coast views • community history.

Distance
Approx. 4km • links with Walk 12.

Time
2–2½ hours.

Difficulty
Easy to moderate • stage 2 to Henry Head unsuitable for wheelchairs.

Access
Anzac Parade buses to La Perouse • street parking.
UBD: Map 296 P14
Gregory's: Map 436 J14.

Facilities
Toilets, shops at La Perouse • picnic spots at beaches and headland. No dogs in national park.

92 ✵ Sydney Strolls ⚓ Eastern Suburbs

Walk 13 Key

- **S** Start
- **1** Old tram loop
- **2** Watchtower
- **3** Lapérouse memorial
- **4** Laperouse Museum
- **5** 'Yarra Bay House'
- **6** Marge Timbery memorial
- **7** National Parks workshop
- **8** Command post
- **9** Henry Head gun emplacements

Despite its rejection by the First Fleeters in 1788, La Perouse acquired some European residents from the 1820s—customs officials, fishermen and, later, the military. Even so, for many decades, most early residents did not come here by choice. There were 19th-century smugglers and gypsies, but the sand dunes, wild weather, swamps, lack of fresh water and poor communications minimised the area's attraction, as did the subsequent location nearby of the infectious diseases hospital and Long Bay Gaol.

In the 1930s Depression, many unemployed and dispossessed families moved to La Perouse's gullies and hillsides. By 1931 more than 350 families—at least 1000 people—were living in tents, humpies and huts made of everything from driftwood, scrap timber, flattened kerosene tins, corrugated iron to hessian bags and bedsteads. Charity, the dole and the New South Wales Golf Club, which extended a pipe to provide a water supply, eased some of the rigours but they were desperate times. Council evictions of the camp began just before World War II, but European migrants and refugees soon began to replace the unemployed, and parts of the camp persisted into the 1950s.

When trams reached here at the beginning of the century, they greatly increased the flow of casual visitors attracted by the scenery, beaches, fort, Pleasure Ground and the Aborigines (see feature box, page 95). A local Aboriginal artefacts industry developed, producing shellwork and moccasins, boomerangs, and other souvenirs. Improved transport also helped spread the suburbs towards, and finally link them to, this outpost on Botany Bay.

This is a walk in two stages beginning at the Anzac Parade bus terminal. Both stages are worth doing and the second stage can easily be linked with Walk 12 (page 85) for a longer, interest-packed walk of three to four hours. Stage one of this walk is a clockwise circuit of the road around the peninsula reserve. Until the 1960s, the bus terminus site was the tram terminus, known as **'the loop'** ❶. Within the tram loop was a kiosk, and, on weekends, Aboriginal artefacts stalls and boomerang-throwing demonstrations. The tram loop was also the site of the earliest snake shows, beginning around 1910 with Professor Fox, who often let himself be bitten to demonstrate his own antidote. It worked well until he made one fatal mistake in Calcutta in 1914. There were other snake showmen, but none as famous as George Cann who presented his shows from the 1920s until his death (of natural causes) in 1965. Son George continues the family tradition on Sundays across the road in the snake enclosure decorated with Aboriginal art murals.

Facing away from the city, follow Anzac Parade south. To the east is Congwong Bay, with Henry Head projecting out beyond—both are part of the second stage of the walk. The valley and hillside back behind Congwong Bay Beach were part of Happy Valley where evicted or unemployed families settled in shacks during the 1930s Depression. The elegant clubhouse of the New South Wales Golf Club controls the heights above as it did then. The course, which opened in 1928, it is now one of several courses which occupy much of the coastal plateau. To the west, the octagonal castellated

Watchtower ❷ was built between 1820 and 1822 on Governor Macquarie's orders to keep a watch on smugglers. Later it became our first customs house and, in 1868, the first La Perouse school, serving the families of local fishermen, customs officials, the military and the Aboriginal mission.

As the roadway turns, Bare Island Fort projects south into Botany Bay. This thoroughly fortified island at the end of an elderly pedestrian bridge, was transformed between 1881 and 1889 to protect Sydney's back door from invasion, the fort designed by British expert, Sir Peter Scratchley. Construction was supervised by Government Architect James Barnet, but the standard of work was poor and contributed to Barnet's resignation. Regarded in military terms as a deathtrap, the fort initially housed five large rifled muzzle-loading guns and a garrison, but by 1912 it had been abandoned. The barracks inside the windswept little island soon became Australia's first War Veterans' Home, a role it retained until 1963. In 1967 the island was taken over by the National Parks and Wildlife Service, which provides organised tours on weekends.

Apart from the names La Perouse and Frenchman's Bay, the six-week visit by the two ships of Comte de Lapérouse (see Walk 11, page 78), which began only six days after the arrival of the First Fleet in January 1788, is well commemorated. The columnar **monument ❸** erected by France in 1828 to commemorate the visit stands within the park area encircled by Anzac Parade. Closer to this area's centre, the **Laperouse Museum ❹**
concentrates on the life, voyages and disappearance of the aristocratic navigator. The museum is housed in the beautifully restored cable station, built in 1882 (and enlarged in 1890) to service the 2528-kilometre telegraphic submarine cable laid from La Perouse to New Zealand in 1876. From early this century until 1987, the building was used as a refuge for women and children. Nearby lies a tomb erected in 1828 atop the grave of Father Receveur, who was with Lapérouse. All these sites have long been centres of French 'pilgrimage' in Australia.

To the north-west, a seawall protecting the Port Botany container depot projects massively out into the bay, an encroachment on much the same scale as the airport runways further around. The beach area below is Frenchmans Bay and the large house visible above is **'Yarra Bay House' ❺**, built in 1903 as a second cable station, and re-established by the local Aboriginal Land Council as a community centre in 1985. The headland beyond Frenchmans Bay conceals both Yarra Bay itself and the site of the popular Yarra Bay Pleasure Grounds which operated from 1901 to the 1950s. Follow Anzac Parade past Endeavour Avenue and the shops to return almost to the starting point. Before the T-junction, look in the central park area for the small roadside memorial to **Marge Timbery ❻**, an outstanding member of the La Perouse Aboriginal community.

Having returned to where you began, you can continue to stage two of the walk. Head across Anzac Parade towards Congwong Bay and take the well-signposted steps beside the toilet block down

La Per

The Aboriginal community has been the most significant and lasting one in 'La Per'. The Muruoradial people, who watched Cook, Phillip and Lapérouse sail into Botany Bay were mostly gone by the 1850s—victims of disease, force and dispossession. However, in 1881, 26 dispossessed South Coast Aborigines moved to La Perouse and a new community began, and persisted. In 1894 the first church mission was established, and in the following year a small area was gazetted by the government as an Aboriginal Reserve. Although treated as curiosities by daytrippers, the community developed (and retains) strong, stable and close links, as well as appropriate activities to benefit from the daytrippers. Their housing was slowly improved over time and most of it moved back from the shifting sands of the beachfront to higher ground. The 1930s Depression brought more Aboriginal people, and shacks developed again in sandy 'Frog Hollow' in front of Frenchmans Bay.

When suburbia reached La Perouse in the 1950s the little Aboriginal community was soon all but surrounded by new housing. The new suburbanites' concerns about their own housing values led to governments at last undertaking some worthwhile improvements to Aboriginal housing conditions. This process continued with the creation of the local Land Council and greater support for Aboriginal projects, the effect of which can easily be seen in the homes of the community today.

La Per schoolchildren head homewards past the century-old Aboriginal Evangelical Church.

to the natural setting of Congwong Bay Beach. At its far end, across the tiny stream that provided Captain Cook with his first reliable fresh water supply in 1770, there are two track heads. One track leads to Little Congwong Beach—which seems to have become a nude-bathing beach—while the path you should take to Henry Head turns left immediately alongside the creek. Beginning as a broad fire trail, this well-marked track climbs for 200 metres and then turns right onto an excellent narrower walking track. After about 450 metres of crossing rocky creek heads and paralleling a road, the track turns at the back of a large **national parks workshop** (7) and meanders south before climbing above Little Congwong Beach. This is a lovely walk, especially in spring, with native vegetation providing an ever-changing display of coast shrublands and wildflowers including mallee, wattles and tea-tree, as well as banksias, bottlebrush and angophora.

The track climbs to ridge-top heathland and, just after an incoming road joins from the left, there is a very large World War II **command post** (8), complete with steel blast windows. Another 300 metres downhill, the track—almost encased at times in native shrubs—joins a surfaced roadway which leads right onto the rock platforms above Henry Head.

Henry Head (9) is a military site from two eras—World War II superimposed on the 1880s and 1890s. Part of the oldest is encountered first, an inclined path dropping into an underground brick and masonry circular gun emplacement and complex. The gun pit was apparently roofed during World War II. Over near the small lighthouse is a covered World War II concrete gun emplacement. Below it, steps drop into an impressive and easily explored 1890s underground complex, the main tunnel of which emerges into a gun pit similar to the first, though this time with no added roof.

The 1890s Henry Head guns operated in conjunction with Bare Island Fort to protect the entrance to Botany Bay and deter landing forces. Both guns here were 6-inch BLs (breach-loaders) on hydro-pneumatic mounts. When they were about to fire, the gun crew pumped up pressure in the mounts which raised the level of the gun above the walls. Upon firing, the recoil drove the gun back down again out of sight (see Walk 6, page 45). The well-constructed old battery was abandoned by the 1930s, but with Australia in serious danger in 1941, the site was hastily put back into use, though this time with two superseded 18-pounder field guns on the clifftops. Two ancient Hotchkiss quick-firing 3-pounder guns were placed at Bare Island to assist in deterring small ships such as landing craft or torpedo boats. Later in the war, covered gun emplacements were built for the Henry Head guns, but as the barrels did not extend beyond the roofline, firing them was earsplitting for the gun crews. By 1944, with the threat of invasion receding, Henry Battery ceased being operational and became a Depot Battery, providing men for other batteries as required.

Henry Head is a lovely spot to sit and enjoy the views or have a picnic lunch. From the head, the downward-leading track to the east can easily be found to pick up Walk 12 if you wish to continue in that direction. Otherwise, when you are ready, simply retrace your steps to Anzac Parade and the end of the walk.